LOURDES COLLEGE LIBRARY

3 0379 1001 3307 5

DUNS SCOTUS LIBRARY
LOURDES COLLEGE
SYLVANIA, OHIO

448
B14

SIGNPOSTS

FRENCH

Edith Baer and
Margaret Wightman

Cambridge University Press

Cambridge

London   New York   New Rochelle

Melbourne   Sydney

063865

2 copies in OhioLink

Published by the Press Syndicate of the University of Cambridge
The Pitt Building, Trumpington Street, Cambridge CB2 1RP
32 East 57th Street, New York, NY 10022, U S A
296 Beaconsfield Parade, Middle Park, Melbourne 3206, Australia

© Cambridge University Press 1982

First published 1982

Printed in Hong Kong by
Wing King Tong

ISBN 0 521 28192 X

Acknowledgements
The photographs in this book were taken by the authors in France,
except for the *Métropolitain* photograph on p 42 supplied by the
French Government Tourist Office.

What this book is about

* It helps you – even if you're a beginner – to understand the signs and notices that will confront you on a visit to France.
* It shows you how to get the gist of them without having to worry about the meaning of every single word.
* It contains plenty of practice material so that you can check your progress.
* It gives you an idea how the French language works.
* It provides some unusual and unexpected insights into the French way of life.

How the book works

'Finding your way through the forest of signs' gives you some general ideas on how to make sense of signs and on how to judge whether they're important to you or not. This part includes notes about the way the language on signs works, and tells you which words to look out for and how to sort out the different types of sign.

Chapters 1—14 deal with situations you may have to cope with and the signs you're likely to come across. Each chapter has a 'Key words' section, listing those words you'll find most useful, explanations of important signs and 'Test yourself' questions for self-checking. For easy reference and revision there's a word list on p 100.

How to use it

* First go carefully through 'The forest of signs'. You can then take the individual chapters in any order; they're self-contained. You may find it a help to re-read 'The forest of signs' before tackling a new chapter.
* Once you've studied the 'Key words' of the chapter, try to memorise them. Then go on to the section introducing the signs. Concentrate on getting the gist as you would need to in a real-life situation – resist the temptation of puzzling out every word.
* Finally try the 'Test yourself' questions at the end of the chapter and check your answers with the Key on p 97.

CONTENTS

FINDING YOUR WAY THROUGH THE FOREST OF SIGNS

In France most areas of public life are well signposted. There are signs to warn you, to ask you to do – or not to do – something, to help you on your way and generally inform you. Signs often flash by and you need to 'get the message' quickly. Many are written in a style of language that you won't meet in everyday speech or want to use yourself. A dictionary won't always help, but guessing often will. But there are pitfalls! (See p 8.)

To try and understand every word on a sign or notice can be a waste of effort, so you need to develop a special technique to pick out the essentials.

1 Concentrate on short bold signs

centre ville (town centre)
entrée des visiteurs (visitors' entrance)

What appears in smaller print is often less important.

access to the castle
is prohibited to animals

2 Sort out the different types of sign

Signs with ! or **attention** (beware) urge you *to take care*
attention enfants (beware – children)

Signs that start with **prière de** or include **s.v.p.** (= **s'il vous plaît**) both meaning 'please', are *polite requests*
  prière de garder le silence (please be quiet)
  s.v.p. fermez les portes (please close the doors)

Signs that begin with words ending in . . .**ez** or . . .**er** ask you *to do* something
  sortez lentement (drive out slowly)
  s'adresser à la caisse (ask at the cash desk)

Signs with **ne pas** or **ne** . . . **pas** (don't) tell you *not to do* something
  ne traversez pas (don't cross)
  ne pas fumer (no smoking)

Signs with **défense de, interdiction de** or **interdit** *forbid you* to do something
    défense d'entrer (entry prohibited)
    passage interdit (no way through)
    interdiction de marcher sur la pelouse (walking on the grass prohibited)

TEST YOURSELF (Answers on p 97)

Which signs (i) ask you to do something (ii) request you politely to do something (iii) tell you not to do something (iv) forbid you to do something (v) remind you to take care?

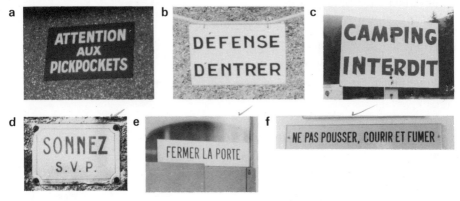

a   ATTENTION AUX PICKPOCKETS

b   DÉFENSE D'ENTRER

c   CAMPING INTERDIT

d   SONNEZ S.V.P.

e   FERMER LA PORTE

f   · NE PAS POUSSER, COURIR ET FUMER ·

3 Pick out the 'key words'

This will often help you to decide whether a sign concerns you or not. For instance, if you want to find your way to the sea front, a sign with **mer** (sea) on it is of interest (the others you can ignore); the same if you were looking for the market (**marché**).

A key word can often help you to sort out the meaning of words linked to it, e.g.
    front de mer (sea front)
    place du marché (market square)

Other words you may be able to pick out are the ones that belong to the same 'family' e.g. **fermez** or **fermer** (close . . .!), **fermé** (closed), **fermeture** (closing).

Many words you don't have to worry about: you can guess their meaning because they are near to, or identical with, an English word, e.g.
    caravanes (caravans)
    entrée (entrance or entry)
    priorité (priority or right of way)

but there are many French words that are 'false friends' (**faux amis**). They look like English words but mean something entirely different, e.g.

car (coach)
cave (wine cellar or wine shop)
essence (petrol)

Words ending in . . .**tion** are particularly treacherous. Some mean practically the same in French and English e.g. **consultation, information, réception, réservation, section**. Others don't, e.g.

circulation (traffic)
déviation (diversion)
exposition (exhibition)
location (hire, letting)
promotion (special offer)
station (taxi rank, petrol station)

Key words are listed at the beginning of each chapter; 'faux amis' are highlighted.

4 Look for other words that matter

They can also give you a clue what a sign is about and help you to decide whether it affects you or not. Try to memorise the words below — they appear on many signs

* **animaux** (animals), **chiens** (dogs): you can ignore the sign unless you have an animal with you or the sign is on someone's front gate (then it's a warning)
    chien méchant (fierce dog)
    accès interdit aux animaux (animals not admitted)

* **appuyez** or **appuyer** (press) appears on many machines and on signs asking you to press a button or bell
    appuyer sur le bouton rouge (press the red button)
    appuyez doucement (press gently)

* **droite** (right), **gauche** (left)
    serrez à droite (keep right)
    1ère rue à gauche (1st street on the left)

* **fermé** means a place is closed, **ouvert** that it's open
    nos bureaux sont ouverts (our offices are open)
    fermé le lundi (closed on Monday)

* **ici** (here) alerts you to where you get something or should do something
  * **en vente ici** (on sale here)
  * **prendre la file ici** (queue here)
* **libre** (free) tells you that something is available or is free of charge
  * **chambres libres** (rooms available)
  * **entrée libre** (entry free of charge or feel free to look around)
  * *but* **libre service** means self-service *not* service free of charge
* **s'adresser** tells you that you have to call elsewhere
  * **s'adresser à l'hôtel** (ask in the hotel)
* **sauf** (except) and **sauf aux** (except for) appear on many road signs exempting certain users
  * **sauf bus** (except buses)
  * **sauf aux livraisons** (except for delivery services)
* **sortie** shows you the way out
* **votre** concerns something belonging to you; **vous** means 'you'
  * **gardez votre ticket sur vous** (keep your ticket on you)

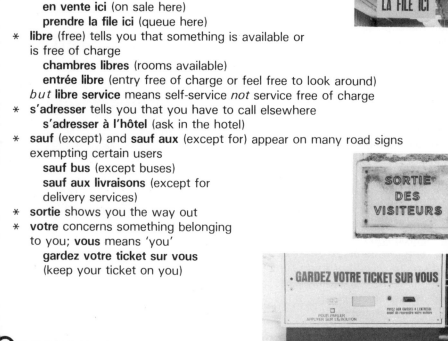

🅿 TEST YOURSELF

Which of these signs would concern you if you (i) wanted to find the exit (ii) were looking for a petrol station that's open (iii) wanted to enter someone's front gate (iv) wanted to drive straight on (v) wanted to park to attend a church service (vi) were smoking (vii) wanted to go to an exhibition?

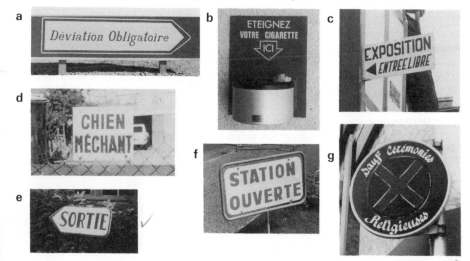

5 Look at the way the 'sign' language works

Remember, especially when deciphering
short signs, that French *word order* is
often the opposite to English usage, e.g.
   WC publics (public loos)
   signal automatique (automatic signal)

Nouns joined by **de** (of) make better
sense if you reverse the order and forget
about **de**
   location de voitures (hire of cars, i.e. car hire)
   jour de marché (day of market, i.e. market day)

Instructions

* The majority of signs telling you *what* to do
  begin with a word in . . .**ez**, . . .**er**, occasionally
  in . . .**re**, . . .**ir**. Exception: **faites** (make)
     entrez sans frapper (enter without knocking)
     introduire 1F (insert 1 franc)
     faites votre choix (make your choice)
* If you're asked *not* to do something
  the first word is generally **ne**
     ne stationnez pas ⎫
     ne pas stationner ⎭ (don't park)

* If you're being told *how* to do
  something the sign usually starts
  with **pour** (= in order to) and the
  instruction comes third
     pour entrer sonnez (to enter − ring)
     pour parler appuyez sur le bouton
     (to speak − press the button)

Prohibitions

* On short signs ending in **interdit** the first word or words say *what* you
  mustn't do
     baignade interdite (bathing prohibited)
* On signs beginning with **interdiction/défense de** (prohibition), **il est interdit/il
  est défendu de** (it is forbidden to) it's the next word that tells you; it usually
  ends in . . .**er**, sometimes . . .**re**, . . .**ir**
     interdiction de tourner à gauche (turning left prohibited)
     il est défendu de traverser les voies (it is forbidden to cross the rails)
* To discover *who* isn't allowed to do something look for **aux** . . .
     interdit aux moins de 16 ans
     (prohibited for people under 16)

olite requests

* If they begin with **prière de** (please) or include **prié de** or **d'** (requested to) the next word is *what* you're asked to do

    prière de fermer la porte (please close the door)

    les visiteurs sont priés d'attendre ici (visitors are requested to wait here)
* If you're requested *not* to do something you'll have to look further to find out what it is

    prière de ne pas stationner devant la porte (please do not park in front of the gate)

TEST YOURSELF

What are you told to do — or not to do? (Don't try to make sense of every word.)

a *Pour visiter s'adresser Porte Royale*

b LE CLIENT EST PRIE D'ATTENDRE UNE VENDEUSE ICI

c INTERDICTION DE FUMER

d SORTIE VÉHICULES NE PAS STATIONNER MERCI

e PRIERE DE FERMER LA PORTE S.V.P.

f NE TRAVERSEZ PAS

Recognise different forms of the same word

In the vocabulary, words are given in their basic form, except where there are important variations.

* An **s**, sometimes **x**, at the end of a word usually tells you it's plural

    jour (day) **jours** (days)   **bureau** (office) **bureaux** (offices)
* Adjectives often add an extra . . .**e**, . . .**s**, . . .**es** or an accent

    station ouverte (petrol station open)

    nos bureaux sont ouverts (our offices are open)

    service routier (road service)

    circulation routière (road traffic)

    Some change more radically, e.g. **tous** (all)

    tous véhicules (all vehicles)   **toutes les chambres** (all the rooms)

    The words for 'old' and 'beautiful' have quite distinct forms — **vieux** and **vieil(le)**, **beau** and **bel(le)**

    vieux port (old harbour)

    vieille ville (old town)

    beau panorama } (beautiful view)
    belle vue

Vieux Port

* You'll come across various forms for 'the' (**le, la, l', les**), for 'of the', (**du, de la, de l', des**) and for 'to the','for the' (**au, à la, à l', aux**).
* On many signs the accents are left off. For instance you'll see **entrée** and **entree, accès** and **acces**. In practice this seldom leads to confusion – but watch out for **ferme**: it can mean 'farm' or be the word for 'closed' with the accent left off. In the text of this book accents are always used.

7 Other things you need to recognise

Days of the week

lundi	Monday	**vendredi**	Friday
mardi	Tuesday	**samedi**	Saturday
mercredi	Wednesday	**dimanche**	Sunday
jeudi	Thursday		

Look out for expressions with **jour** (day)
jours fériés public holidays (also called **fêtes**)   **jour de marché** market day
jours ouvrables working days   **tous les jours** every day

Numbers

1st, 2nd, 3rd etc. appear as 1er, 1ère or 1e, 2ème or 2e, 3ème or 3e; when they refer to centuries they look like this: XVème or XVe (15th), XIXème or XIXe (19th).
The figures 1 and 7 are often handwritten 1 and 7.
An **m** after a number means 'metres' (not miles),
    100m = 100 metres
After a road, house number etc. **bis** (secondary) means 'a'
    2**bis** = 2a

Times

The 24-hour system is in use everywhere; 'hour' appears as **h** or **heure**, half an hour is ½**h** or **demi-heure**, 2 hours **2 heures** etc.
    12.00, 12h, 1200 (or **midi**)   12 noon (or midday)
    00.00, 24h, 2400 (or **minuit**)   12 midnight
    19.30, 19h30   7.30pm
    24h/24 means around the clock service

Money

Prices can be written in several ways: **franc** = **f, F, fr.** or **frs**;
centimes = **cts., c., 0. ..** or **0 fr. ..**
    2f50, 2F50, 2,50F, 2fr.50   ½F, ½f or **0,50, 0fr50, 50cts.**

8 Get to know these four-letter words . . .

avec with	**pour** for, in order to
dans in	**sans** without
hors out of	**vers** towards

. . . these three-letter and two-letter words

par by, via	**en** in
sur for, on	**et** and
	ou or

1 GETTING AROUND ON FOOT

KEY WORDS

entrée (way in)	**entrer, entrez** tell you to go in
passage (way through)	**passage interdit** (no way through) **passage souterrain** (subway, underpass)
piétons (pedestrians)	**piétonne, piétonnier** (for pedestrians) as in **rue piétonne, voie piétonne, zone piétonne, espace piétonnier** (pedestrian precinct)
sortie (way out)	**sortie de secours** (emergency exit)
ville (town)	**centre ville** (town centre) **hôtel de ville** (town hall)
voie (way, road)	**voie piétonne** (pedestrian precinct) **voie sans issue** (dead end)

Finding your way

Look for navy on off-white or black on white direction signs to find particular places such as the town centre (**centre ville** or **centre**), harbour (**port**), beach (**plage**)

or important buildings e.g. the town hall (**mairie** or **hôtel de ville**), station (**gare**), post office (**poste** or **PTT**, short for **Postes, Télécommunications, Télédiffusion**), the sports centre (**stade** or **palais des sports**), a castle (**château**).

For shopping areas look for **centre commercial**, **marché** (market) or **halles** (covered market).

SNCF = French Railways (see p 43)

Street names also help you find your way around. A street or road may be marked **avenue, ave., boulevard, bld., bd., chemin** or **rue**; **quai** tells you that it's along a waterfront. A square is named **place** or **pl.**, a circus or roundabout **rond-point**.

13

Routes for pedestrians

You recognise them by the word **piétons**, occasionally **pédestre**

but when **piétons** is at the head of a sign, pedestrians are usually told what to do.

emprunter use
trottoir pavement
opposé opposite

Piétonne, **piétonnier** or this symbol tell you that it's a pedestrian precinct.

Walking in the right direction

You may be told to turn left (**à gauche**) or right (**à droite**) or to go straight on (**tout droit**).

crêperie pancake-house
glaces ices
salon de thé tea room

Sometimes you're asked to call elsewhere.

Crossing the road

Many traffic lights for pedestrians show the words **passez** (go) and **attendez** (wait).

When you see this notice you have to press (**appuyez**) a button (**bouton**) and wait for the 'green' (**le vert**), i.e. the green sign for pedestrians.

PIETONS ⊙
POUR TRAVERSER
APPUYEZ
SUR CE BOUTON

ET ATTENDEZ
LE VERT
PIETONS

traverser to cross   **ce** this

Going into places

The entrance may be marked **entrée** or there may be a sign directing you to it.

ENTRÉE A L'AUTRE PORTE

autre other   **porte** door

Where you see **poussez** or **pousser** you push the door open, where it says **tirez** or **tirer** you pull. Sometimes a sign invites you to enter without knocking (**sans frapper**). Doors to many buildings — blocks of flats, banks, offices — are kept locked and you may be asked to ring (**sonnez** or **sonner**).

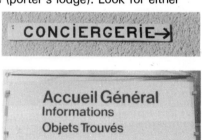

SONNEZ - ENTREZ

If you want to get into your hotel late at night see if there's a **sonnette de nuit** (night bell).

A special feature of French blocks of flats and other buildings is the **concierge** (caretaker, usually a woman) or **conciergerie** (porter's lodge). Look for either sign if you're not sure how to get into a building or to the flat or office you want.

CONCIERGERIE→

Elsewhere there may be a reception office — **bureau d'accueil**, just **bureau** (office) or **accueil** (welcome), or **réception**.

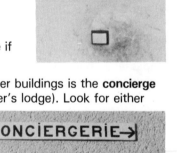

Accueil Général
Informations
Objets Trouvés

objets trouvés lost property

Getting around inside buildings . . .

The various floors are called **étage**, except for the ground floor (**rez-de-chaussée**) and the basement (**sous-sol**). To get there you may need to find the stairs (**escalier**) or the lift (**ascenseur**).

ASCENSEUR

Besides **bureau**, words to help you around inside buildings include **cabinet** (office, e.g. of a solicitor), **direction** (management), **salle** (large room, hall).

. . . and out again

Look for **sortie**.

If you see a sign with **fermez** or **fermer**, close the door behind you.

Watch how you go

Avoid going where it says **interdit** coupled with **accès**, **entrée**, **passage** or **pelouse** (lawn)

or **défense de** or **d'**

or **privé** (private).

There's no point going down a road marked **sans issue** (without exit) or **impasse** — that's what the French call a cul-de-sac!

Take care where it says **attention**.

SALLE _au_ 1ᵉ ETAGE

SORTIE PAR L'ESCALIER

ACCÈS PIETONS INTERDIT

DANGER DÉFENSE D'ENTRER DANS LE CHANTIER

chantier building site

COUR PRIVEE

cour yard

CHEMIN SANS ISSUE

ATTENTION A LA MARCHE

marche step

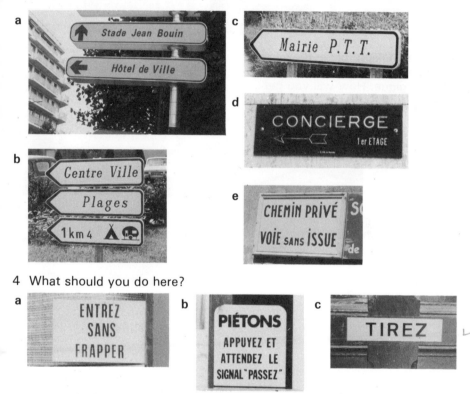

❓ TEST YOURSELF

Before you attempt the questions go over the chapter again and 'The forest of signs' section as well.

1 Identify these 'faux amis': **cabinet   défense   issue   quai**

2 These look deceptively alike. What's the difference between them?
(i) **à droite   tout droit** (ii) **marche   marché** (iii) **place   plage**
(iv) **port   porte**

3 Where do these signs direct you to?

a

Stade Jean Bouin

Hôtel de Ville

c

Mairie P.T.T.

d

CONCIERGE
1er ÉTAGE

b

Centre Ville

Plages

1km 4

e

CHEMIN PRIVÉ
VOIE sans ISSUE

4 What should you do here?

a

ENTREZ
SANS
FRAPPER

b

PIÉTONS
APPUYEZ ET
ATTENDEZ LE
SIGNAL "PASSEZ"

c

TIREZ

5 If you're on foot which of these signs affect you? What are you asked *not* to do?

a

PELOUSE
INTERDITE

b

DEFENSE D'ENTRER
A
TOUS VEHICULES

c

ATTENTION
à la Barrière
Passage Piétons
INTERDIT

6 Where would you go to find the loo?

a 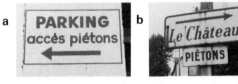 b

7 When would you find these signs for pedestrians helpful?

a  b c

8 You're looking for (a) the car park
   (to collect your car) (b) the Rue
   de Belgique. How will you get
   there?

a

b

9 This sign has an important
   message. What is it?

Innocent abroad:

18

2 MOTORING

(a) Going the right way

circulation (traffic)	circulation routière (road traffic)
itinéraire (route)	itinéraire bis (secondary route) itinéraire conseillé (alternative route)
priorité (right of way)	prioritaire (something that has right of way)
route (road, way)	general word for road, shortened to **Rte** autoroute (motorway) route express (long-distance expressway) routier (road . . .)
sens (direction)	refers to the flow of traffic: contresens (opposite direction) sens interdit (no entry) sens unique (one-way)
voie (road, one lane of a road)	voie de droite (right hand lane) voie unique (single-lane road) *but* voie piétonne is a pedestrian precinct

OTHER IMPORTANT WORDS

enfants (children)   piétons (pedestrians)
poids lourds or PL (heavy or long vehicles)
(poids = weight   lourds = heavy)

Hiring a car

If you want to hire a car look for
location de voitures
(**location** = hire *not* location)

Remember: **voitures** means cars; road
signs for cars sometimes say **autos**
instead but *never* **cars** — that's short for
autocars and means coaches.

SNCF = French Railways (see p 43)

The colour of direction signs

Off-white background: for most roads; the number on
the sign gives you the distance in kilometres, the
small panel above it the road number — **N** or **RN** on
red (**route nationale**) for a trunk road, **D** on yellow
(**route départementale**) for a main road.

19

Green background: for major routes
between large towns.
Yellow background: for a traffic diversion.
Blue background: for motorways and
roads leading to them.

Special direction signs to avoid congestion

Green arrows and signs indicate an
alternative route (**itinéraire bis**) avoiding
congested main roads.

Orange arrows and signs indicate a
short relief road (**délestage**) round a
particular bottleneck.

During summer holiday periods you
can get details of these routes and
traffic information at roadside kiosks
marked **bison futé** (clever Red Indian)
or with this sign.

carte map   **gratuite** free

The rule of the road

Priority

Most road sign symbols are the same as
in Britain. This one (yellow on white) is
an important exception. It means
you're on a priority road. A dark blue
line through it marks the end of the
priority road.
Traffic from the right has priority at
junctions when there's no priority sign;
there may be a sign to remind you.

Watch out also for signs with **passage**
(right of way *not* passage). You have to
give way at a junction when it says
cédez le passage, but you have right of
way at crossroads where there's a sign
passage protégé.

There are occasionally signs beginning
with **vous avez** . . . telling you that you
have priority or with **vous n'avez
pas**. . .saying that you haven't.

protégé protected

20

Prioritaire and **priorité au** or **aux** warn you about other road users who have right of way. This sign on the back of a bus tells you not to overtake it as it pulls away from its stop (**son arrêt**).

en quittant on leaving   **ce** this

Slow lane

On the open road drivers of slow vehicles (**véhicules lents**) are often told to keep to the right hand lane (**voie de droite**) – it includes you if you're towing a caravan.

Tolls

You may have to pay a toll (**péage**) to go through a road tunnel or cross a particular bridge (**pont**). Tolls are also payable on most motorways. (For more details see p 32, 33)

To avoid busy towns

Look for **rocade** or **voie de rocade** (by-pass) or **périphérique** (ring road) or follow the sign **poids lourds** (you can easily mistake it for the place name **Lourdes**!). It marks a detour for large or heavy vehicles avoiding narrow or congested streets – useful if you're towing a caravan. These routes are sometimes signposted with a lorry symbol and **itinéraire conseillé** or **recommandé** (alternative route).

sud south

Driving in towns

The (navy on off-white) sign at the beginning of a town or village gives you its name and the road number. It acts as a speed limit sign (60 kilometres per hour or 35 mph in a built-up area).

At the end of a town a similar sign with a diagonal red line through it ends the speed restriction.

21

To get to the town centre follow **centre** or **centre ville; toutes directions** (all routes) will take you out of town again.

Follow **autres directions** (all other routes) if your destination isn't mentioned on a sign.

rive bank

In some towns you may see **onde verte** (green wave) with a recommended speed. At this speed you'll meet all traffic lights on that road at green.

files lanes

Looking for particular buildings or places
(see chapter 1, p 13)

Roads that are closed or restricted

Route barrée tells you that the road is closed.

à 100m 100 metres ahead

Some roads are prohibited to certain types of vehicle, such as **poids lourds**, **caravanes**, vehicles with trailers (**remorques**) etc.

Don't go where you see **circulation interdite** — no traffic is allowed at all — or **sens interdit** (no entry)
but **sens unique** means one-way street, usually marked with a white arrow on blue.
Impasse or **sans issue** tells you that it's a dead end.

No entry . . . except for

Many 'no entry' and 'all vehicles prohibited' signs carry words exempting some road users — look for **sauf** . . . (except). You could be an exception if you're visiting a resident (**riverain**).

But **livraisons** is unlikely to include you — it's for delivery services and tradesmen; nor is **desserte locale** — it refers to local services.

Things you're requested to do

Remember that the word telling you what to do usually ends in . . .**ez** (see p 10).

  ralentissez (slow down)
  roulez lentement (drive slowly)
  roulez au pas (dead slow)
  (**au pas** = at walking pace)
  entrez . . . (drive in), **sortez** . . . (drive out)
  serrez à droite/à gauche (keep right/left)
  allumez vos feux de croisement
  (switch on your headlights)

but **feux** can also be short for **feux tricolores** (traffic lights); **feu clignotant** is a flashing light.

Watch out for . . .

* **vitesse** (speed): it usually implies that you should drive slowly.

ni . . . ni
neither . . . nor
bruit noise

* **rappel** (reminder): on its own or with a number it reminds you that a speed limit is in force, but it also appears on other signs.

* **sortie** on a warning sign: this alerts you to vehicles or people emerging, e.g. **camions** (lorries), **usine** (factory), **école** (school).

* **accôtement** (verge): don't drive on to the verge where you see **impraticable** or **non stabilisé** — it may give way.

* **carrefour** (crossroads): any mention of it means you should approach it with care *but* don't be misled by signs pointing to the hypermarket called **Carrefour**!

* **chaussée deformée** (bad road surface)

* **travaux** (works): you are warned of road works ahead. When you come to the end of them there may be a sign with **fin de chantier** (end of road works).

* **aire**: nothing to do with 'air' — it's a lay-by; some are named after a locality, others are called **aire de repos** (**repos** = rest).

If you need roadside assistance

Look out for roadside phones with **secours routier** (roadside assistance) and signs with **gendarmerie** (police). (See also p 94, 95.)

❷ TEST YOURSELF

1 Identify these 'faux amis':
   circulation   carte   déviation   passage   route   sens

2 Why do you need to be careful here?

3 Where do these signs take you to?

4 What is the message of these signs?

a **SENS INTERDIT À 100m.**

b **FIN DE SENS UNIQUE**

c **20 VOIE UNIQUE**

5 What are you supposed to do here?

a **CÉDEZ LE PASSAGE**

b **ENTREZ LENTEMENT OBSERVEZ LE SILENCE PAS DE BRUIT SVP**

c **DANGER CHAUSSÉE DÉFORMÉE SUR — 7 KMS RALENTISSEZ RISQUE NIDS DE POULE**

6 Who has right of way here?

a **PRIORITE AUX PIETONS**

b **VOUS N'AVEZ PAS LA PRIORITÉ**

7 If you're towing a caravan what do these signs tell you?

a **CARS VÉHICULES UTILITAIRES CARAVANES**

b **ITINÉRAIRE RECOMMANDÉ**

8 Suppose you want to drive to Lisieux, Brest, or Paris. What information do these signs provide?

a **DÉLESTAGE 400 m LISIEUX**

b **BREST Par Rᵗᵉ Express**

c **DUNKERQUE Sᵗ OMER ARRAS par Centre Ville BOULOGNE PARIS par N.1**

063865

(b) Finding somewhere to park

KEY WORDS

parc (park, car park)	**parc auto, parc de stationnement** (car park) **parcmètre** (parking meter) **parcotrain** (car park for commuters)
parking (car park)	**parking souterrain** (underground car park)
stationner (to park)	**stationnement, stat^t.** (parking)

OTHER IMPORTANT WORDS

gratuit ⎱ free
libre ⎰

payant (you have to pay)

SYMBOLS WORTH KNOWING

parking fee required
(navy on white)

parking disc required
(navy on white)

Most other symbols for parking and no-parking are the same as in Britain.

Names of different types of vehicle

Useful if you want to know whether a parking restriction applies to you or not.

Four-wheelers

autocars de tourisme excursion coaches
cars short for **autocars** coaches
poids lourds, PL heavy or long vehicles
véhicules utilitaires commercial vehicles
voitures de location hire cars
voitures de tourisme private cars

Two-wheelers (2 roues − roue = wheel)

bicyclettes ⎱
cycles ⎬ bicycles
vélos ⎰
cyclos = cyclomoteurs motorised cycles
motos = motocycles motorcycles
vélomoteurs mopeds

Street parking

* Look for the P symbol (white on navy), but check if other words on the sign limit parking to a particular type of vehicle. You can certainly park your car if it says **voitures** or **tous véhicules** (all vehicles), but not, for instance, if it says **cars**!

légères light   **seulement** only

* Look also for **stationnement**. No problem if it also says **autorisé, toléré** (permissible), or **bilatéral** or **des 2 côtés** (on both sides).

But you can only park on the side where you see **stationnement permanent de ce côté** or **côté de stationnement**.

Limité means you can park, but for a limited time only. **Alterné** tells you that parking is allowed on one side of the road at a time, alternating half-monthly (**semi-mensuel**).

Réglementé warns you that parking regulations are in force. Sometimes you're told to park on the pavement (**sur le trottoir**), maybe with one wheel (**une roue**) or the back wheels (**roues arrière**) on it *but* signs with **2 roues** refer to two-wheelers only.

* Watch out for 'no-waiting' signs that apply only on certain days or at certain times (i.e. you may park at all other times), or in certain places, e.g. where you can park on the pavement but not on the roadway (**chaussée**).

Blue zones

To park in a blue zone (**zone bleue**) you need a parking disc.

You set your time of arrival and display the disc inside the windscreen. Disc parking is usually limited to 1 ½ hours, except over lunchtime.

27

You can get a disc from a **zone bleue** office, sometimes the town hall (**mairie** or **hôtel de ville**) or the local tourist office (**office de tourisme** or **syndicat d'initiative**). Or you can buy one from a tobacconist's (**tabac**) in a **zone bleue**.

This sign should cheer you.

Parking meters

Parcmètres function like parking meters in Britain. Parking is usually charged in units of 20 or 30 minutes; you need ½F and 1F coins (**pièces**). It's free as a rule on Sundays and public holidays.

* Wherever you park it's worth checking if restrictions apply between 12 – 2 pm.

Don't park . . .

* where you see **ne pas stationner**, **parking** or **stationnement interdit**, **défense** or **interdiction de stationner** – unless it says **fin d'interdiction de stationner** (end of 'no parking'!)

* in front of exits or entrances for vehicles – look for **sortie**

propriété property   **cour** yard

* where you see **gênant** (causing obstruction)

* in a **rue** . . ., **voie** . . . or **zone piétonne** (pedestrian precinct)

* where you see **enlèvement** (removal, i.e. towing away) or **enlevé** (removed). You'll have to pay a fine (**amende**) – often a heavy one

Arr. Mun. = **arrêté municipal** bye-law

* where you see a 'no waiting' or 'no stopping' sign unless you're sure any exemption includes you – look for **sauf** . . .

* where parking is private (**privé**) or reserved (**réservé**) for certain purposes, e.g. **livraisons** (deliveries), **marché** (market), or for certain users e.g. **visiteurs**, **occupants** and you're not among the 'privileged'

)ff street parking

Look for **parking, parc auto(s), parc de stationnement** or just the P symbol; **parcotrain** is a car park for commuters. There's no way of knowing in advance if it's open-air or multi-storey, but **souterrain** tells you it's underground.

You have to pay where it says **payant**, but it's free of charge where you see **gratuit** or **libre**. In parts of France parking is free during August (**août**).

places spaces

Paying the fee

Many car parks that are **payant** use the 'pay and display' system. You're told to take (**prenez**) a ticket from a **distributeur** or **horodateur** (ticket machine) and display it inside the windscreen (**pare-brise**).

placer put
façon manner
face interne inner surface

The ticket machine itself is labelled **distributeur de tickets de stationnement**. In multi-storey car parks you often pay the fee into a machine (**caisse automatique**) *before* collecting (**avant de prendre**) your car — so keep your ticket with you.

n'oubliez pas don't forget

How to cope with parking fee machines and where to get change see p 57-8.

❷ TEST YOURSELF

1 Identify these 'faux amis': **cars   cyclos   motos**

2 If you're driving your own car and want to park which would be the right signs?

3 When do you have to pay and when not?

4 It's 3 o'clock on a Saturday afternoon. Can you leave your car at any of these places?

5 Some 'no waiting' signs exempt certain users. What about this one?

6 What is the difference between these signs?

(i) a

PRENEZ
VOTRE TICKET
A
L'HORODATEUR

b

PARKING PAYANT
HORODATEUR →

(ii) a

PARKING
OBLIGATOIRE
2 ROUES

b

P
VOITURES
LÉGÈRES
ROUES ARRIÈRE
AU TROTTOIR

7 What does it say here about parking?

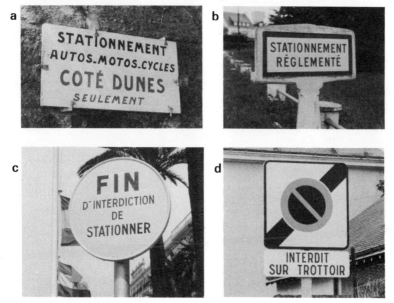

a

STATIONNEMENT
AUTOS.MOTOS.CYCLES
COTÉ DUNES
SEULEMENT

b

STATIONNEMENT
RÉGLEMENTÉ

c

FIN
D'INTERDICTION
DE
STATIONNER

d

INTERDIT
SUR TROTTOIR

(c) Motorway driving

👤 KEY WORDS

aire
(lay-by)

autoroute
(motorway)

péage
(toll)

aire de repos (rest area)
aire de service (service area)

autoroutiers (lorry drivers using the motorway)

How to join the motorway

Look for **autoroute** or the white on blue motorway symbol. Some signs also have A (occasionally B) and the motorway number, others name the places where the motorway leads.

Péage warns you that you have to pay a toll (see below).

These signs direct you to Tours and Ballan Miré by ordinary road and to Paris by motorway.

Coping with tolls

Tolls are charged on most stretches of motorway. Advance warnings say **section à péage à . . .m**. As you approach a toll barrier a sign **péage à . . .m** will tell you how far away it is.

Motorways are managed by different regional companies, so the toll-collecting system varies. You may have to pay as you drive on to or off the motorway, or at barriers at intervals along the motorway. A sign **ticket automatique** means that you have to take a ticket from a machine — you hand it in and pay as you leave the motorway. (**Sortie gratuite** means a toll-free exit.)

At many toll barriers you need to choose the correct lane (**file**). The one marked **automatique** is for car drivers who have the exact money ready — you put it into a chute and the barrier opens automatically.

You're told in advance what coins you'll need. Look for **préparez**. . .

If you haven't the right change, are towing a caravan or driving a vehicle other than a car, take the lane marked **monnaie** (change); it's usually on the right — **à droite** — and you pay the person on duty.

A lane marked **abonnés** is for season ticket holders.

Important signs on the motorway

Croix (cross) indicates an intersection; **bifurcation** (fork) warns you that the motorway divides and you'll have to get into the correct lane.

There are frequent signs for drivers of slow vehicles (**véhicules lents**) to keep to the extreme right hand lane (**voie de droite**) marked off with a thick white broken line (see also p 21).

If you want to rest or eat . . .

Look for the P symbol or **aire de** . . . (lay-by or service area), usually followed by a place name (see also p 24). Advance warnings often tell you how far the next few lay-bys are.

Some motorway lay-bys have picnic facilities and possibly loos (**sanitaires**). Larger ones may have a tourist office (**bureau de tourisme**), a shop selling local produce (**produits régionaux**) and refreshments. A service area, sometimes known as **aire de service** or by a commercial name such as **Restop** or **Restoroute** will have petrol and round-the-clock restaurant facilities.

auto-routiers here means facilities for motorway lorry drivers

. . or to get petrol

Watch out for the petrol pump symbol or a brand name — maybe an unfamiliar one like **Antar** (see above).

If you want to leave the motorway

Exits are not numbered. Signs (navy on white) give the name of the nearest town they lead to. There may be several exits to one town, sometimes identified as **nord** (north), **sud** (south), **est** (east), **ouest** (west) and **centre** (town centre).

Some exits are signposted **sortie**.

If you break down

There is an orange-coloured emergency phone about every two kilometres; it will put you in touch with the motorway police (**service de police** or **gendarmerie autoroute**).

❷ TEST YOURSELF

1 Identify these 'faux amis': **automatique   file   monnaie**

2 What do these signs tell you?

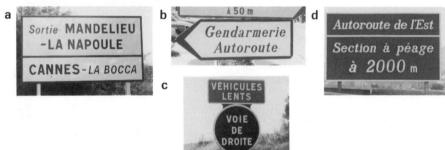

3 You're driving the family saloon and are right out of small change. Which sign is for you? Should you go right or left?

4 How do you interpret this sign?

(d) Going to a service station

KEY WORDS

essence
(petrol)

station   **station service** (service station)
(petrol station)

Finding a service station

A sign pointing to one will probably say
essence or advertise a brand name. **Libre
service**, occasionally **self**, tells you it's a
self-service station.

A service station that's open often displays a sign **station ouverte**. **Dernière
station avant l'autoroute** warns you that it's the last service station before the
motorway.

Filling up the tank

There are two grades of petrol roughly
equivalent to 2-star and 4-star. ✳✳✳✳
is **super** or **supercarburant**, ✳✳ is called
ordinaire, essence auto or **essence** (also
the word for petrol). Prices are quoted
per litre (**prix au litre**) (4.5 litres =
1 gallon).

You normally buy petrol in units of 50
or 100 francs unless you're filling up.

faites le plein fill up

Coping with self-service pumps

Look out for **libre service** or
servez-vous (serve yourself).
Pumps work more or less as in
Britain. You pay at the cash desk
(**caisse**).

Pumps marked **mélange** (mixture) or
2 temps (two stroke) are mainly for
filling up motorbikes and are usually
coin-operated.

appareil apparatus, i.e. pump

35

Oil, air, water

Vidange tells you that you can have your oil changed. If you want it checked look for signs with **huile** (oil).

For air for your tyres, look for **air**. Tyre pressure is measured in kilograms per square centimetre: $1,7 \text{ kg/cm}^2 = 24$ lbs per sq. inch.

For water look for **eau**.

nous sommes we are
niveau level

Getting the car washed . . .

Lavage tells you that you can get your car washed but **lavage libre service** means you have to operate the carwash yourself, i.e. it's coin-operated.

. . . serviced

If your car wants lubricating look for **graissage**; if it needs tuning the sign should say **réglages**.

tôlerie coachwork
peinture paintwork

. . . repaired

Look for a service station or a workshop (**atelier** or **garage**) advertising **réparations** (repairs) or **mécanique** (for anything mechanical *not* a mechanic).

A broken windscreen may be replaced where you see **pare-brise**.

If you have a puncture look for **pneus** (tyres) or **pneu service**; **pneus toutes marques** tells you they sell all makes.

Remember: many service stations close one day a week; a sign with **fermeture hebdomadaire** (weekly closing) will tell you which day.

TEST YOURSELF

1 Identify these 'faux amis': **essence   mécanique   station**

2 Which sign is right if you need

(i)   2-star petrol?

a

mélange **2 temps**

LIBRE SERVICE

PRIX DU [ ] F
POUR 1 FL[ ] L

antar
MELANGE 2 % D'HUILE

b

ESSENCE AUTO
PRIX AU LITRE
3,22

4

Mobil

Essence

(ii)   your oil checked?

a

AIR | EAU

b

et votre
HUILE

(iii)   a tyre mending?

a

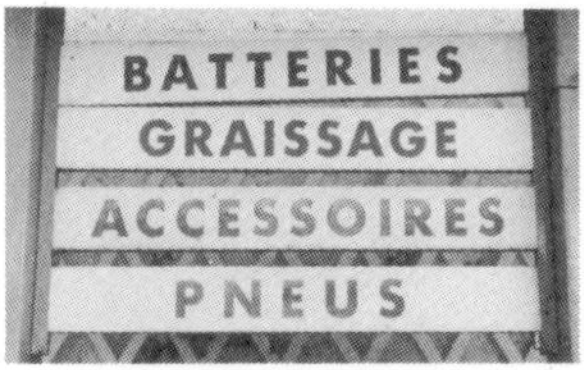

BATTERIES
GRAISSAGE
ACCESSOIRES
PNEUS

b

VIDANGE
GRAISSAGE

(iv)   your car washed?

a

STATION
OUVERTE
Lavage
Graissage
Vidanges
Service Rapide

b

I C I
PARE BRISE
TOUS MODELES

Innocent abroad:

EVEN TELL YOU
WHERE THE AIR'S
GOOD FOR A PICNIC.

AIRE DE
PIQUE NIQUE

3 LOCAL TRANSPORT (See also chapter 4)

🔴 KEY WORDS

arrêt
(stop)

arrêt autobus, arrêt autocar (bus stop)

billets
(tickets)

billet de supplément (supplementary ticket)

carnet
(booklet)

carnet de tickets (book or batch of tickets)

correspondance
(connection)

service en correspondance (connecting service)

routier
(road . . .)

gare routière (coach station)
lignes routières, services routiers (road services)

voyageurs
(passengers)

(a) Going by bus

Different types of bus

Autobus are usually buses for travel inside a town; **autocars** means they also go beyond the town.

Coaches run by **SNCF** (French Railways) to connect with rail services are generally called **cars**.

If you need information about them look for **service routiers** or **lignes routières**.

Other coaches are known as **rapides**, often followed by the name of the area they serve.

If you want the coach station make for **gare routière**.

Touraine Tours region

Getting a ticket

Local transport systems vary. In some towns you can get tickets (**tickets, billets** or **titres de transport**) not only on the buses but also from special kiosks, tobacconists and occasionally machines. A **carnet de tickets** can save you money.

vente sale

38

In some places – Paris especially – you have to cancel (**oblitérer**) your ticket in a machine inside the bus.

Travelling in the right direction

Many stops give the name or initials of the bus company (e.g. **TRT, Courriers Bretons**) but not always the route number (**ligne**).

A place name on a bus stop tells you where you are, not where the bus goes (e.g. **hôtel de ville** means you're at the town hall, *not* going to it!). Look on the front of the bus for the destination. You can often check the bus route on the side of the bus.

av. = avenue   cimetière cemetery   rue street

If you have to signal the driver (**conducteur** or **machiniste**) to make him stop, the sign will say **faire signe au conducteur** or **au machiniste**, or simply **faire signe**.

Getting on or off

If the bus door (**porte**) doesn't open automatically you'll probably have to press a button.

pour ouvrir to open

The entrance is normally at the front and may be marked **entrée** or **montée**. Some buses have two entrances: if you haven't a ticket, get on where you see **sans ticket**, otherwise use the door that says **avec ticket** or **autres voyageurs** (other passengers).

To get off look for **sortie** or **descente**, but *not* **sortie** (or **issue**) **de secours** – that's the emergency exit.

(b) Taking a taxi

Taxi ranks say **taxis** or **station taxis**. To get a taxi go to the head of the rank (**tête de station**), not **fin de station** — that's the opposite end!

Don't be misled by a telephone with **taxiphone** on it: it's nothing to do with taxis (see chapter 6, p 54).

(c) Using the Paris underground

To find an underground station look for **métro, métropolitain** (its old name) or the symbol **M**.

The **métro** shares some stations with the suburban rail network called **RER** (= **réseau express régional**) and with **SNCF**.

Getting a ticket

The Paris transport system is called **RATP** (= **régie autonome des transports parisiens**). In central Paris the same tickets are valid for the underground, buses and **RER** lines. You can buy them from machines at bus stops, at **métro** and **RER** ticket offices and **RATP** kiosks.

If you travel out into the suburbs (**banlieue**) you'll need a supplementary ticket (**billet de supplément** or **billet banlieue**).

Beware: some machines that say **tickets** or **billets** dispense tickets for car parks (see p 29), others change 10F notes (see p 58) and those outside banks marked **distributeur de billets** are automatic cash points.

Travelling in the right direction

To find your way to the platform (**quai**) follow the sign **accès aux quais**.

Métro lines are numbered and are identified by the name of the station at the end of each line. Look for **direction** and a place name.

Pte = **Porte** Gate

If you have to change trains look for **correspondance**, not **sortie** – that will take you out of the station.

❷ TEST YOURSELF

1 Identify these 'faux amis': **correspondance   conducteur   station**

2 You haven't a bus ticket. Which is the correct door?

3 Where does this subway lead to?

4 You're meeting friends in Ivry and are travelling by **métro**. Should you change trains here or leave the station?

5 What types of transport could you get here?

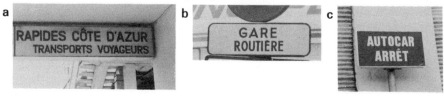

41

d SNCF

Dans la Gare
Restaurant
Le Dolmen
BAR AMERICAN

BRASSERIE
CAFETERIA
SELF SERVICE

METRO

e MÉTROPOLITAIN

6 What kind of tickets
can you buy here?

b BILLETS DE SUPPLÉMENT
POUR LES SECTIONS DE BANLIEUE

a CARNETS de
TICKETS
tarif normal
AUTOBUS
ou METRO

c ~R.A.T.P~

VENTE DES TITRES
DE
TRANSPORT

Innocent abroad:

I WANT A TAXI
TO THE **HOTEL**
NOT THE **STATION**!

STATION
TAXIS

RÉSERVÉ

42

4 GOING BY TRAIN (See also chapter 3)

KEY WORDS

billet
(train ticket)

composter   **composteur** (date-stamping machine)
(to date-stamp)

gare
(station)

quai   **ticket de quai** (platform ticket)
(platform)

voyageur
(passenger)

Getting to the station

Look for **gare** or **gare SNCF** (**SNCF** =
**Société nationale des chemins de fer
français** i.e. French Railways)
but *not* **gare routière** (coach station),
gare maritime (boat terminal) or **aérogare**
(air terminal).
As a rule you recognise a railway station
by this symbol.

Finding out about train times

For the timetable look for **horaires, départs des trains** or **trains au départ**.
Trains to Paris are sometimes listed on a separate board headed **direction Paris**,
long-distance ones on a board called **grandes lignes**. At big stations **trains en
partance** shows which trains are about to depart.

If you're meeting a train see if there's
a notice with **train en provenance de**
(coming from).

Places where you can get train and
travel information have a sign ℹ,
informations or **renseignements**. If you
need general help look for **accueil**
(welcome) or **bureau d'accueil**.

43

Different types of trains

To find the type of train look on the indicator board under **nature**. **TEE** means **Trans-Europ-Express**. A fast train may be a **rapide** or **express**; a high-speed train is **TGV**(= **train à grande vitesse**). A **corail** short for **confort** + **rail**, is an air-conditioned inter-city train, also so called because of its coral-coloured (**corail**) doors and décor.
The daytime motorail service is **train autos-jour (TAJ)**, a car sleeper **train autos-couchettes (TAC)**, *but* **autorail** or **automoteur** is a railcar for local travel.

navette shuttle service
sans arrêt non-stop

Getting a ticket

Make for the counter (**guichet**) marked **billets**. For long-distance travel inside France it may say **grandes lignes**, for travel outside France **pour l'étranger** (for abroad), for local and suburban services **banlieue**.

You can often buy tickets for short journeys or platform tickets from machines marked **distribution automatique**. If you need change a **changeur de monnaie** (coin-changing machine) is usually nearby.

Before going to the platform you must stamp (**composter**) your ticket, even if it's only a platform ticket, in the orange machine called **composteur**.

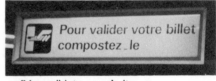

valider validate   **le** it

If it's out of order (**en dérangement** or **hors service**) you'll need to find another machine (**un autre appareil**) or get an official to validate your ticket. Otherwise you may have to pay a fine.

Finding the platform and boarding the train

On some departure boards the platform is called **voie** (line), but to get there follow the sign **quais** or **accès aux quais**. You may be told to use a subway (**passage souterrain**).

44

On the platform there may be a **composition des trains** or **position des voitures**: it shows you the order of the carriages (**voitures**). If you want to smoke look for one marked **fumeurs**, otherwise **non fumeurs**.

Coping with luggage

On most stations there are trolleys (**chariots**). If you want to leave your luggage look for **consigne** (left luggage) or **consigne automatique** (luggage lockers)
but **bagages** is where you send off luggage or large parcels.

choose a locker equipped with a key	choisissez un casier muni de la clef

1 Open the locker and
  put in your luggage
	1 **Ouvrez le casier et
	  placez vos bagages**

2 Put the coins in the
  slot
	2 **Mettez la monnaie dans
	  la fente**

3 Close by pressing
  against the door
  and keep the key
	3 **Fermez en appuyant
	  sur la porte et
	  conservez la clef**

When you collect your luggage and it says **repayez** you have to pay again.

Facilities at stations

Salle d'attente is a waiting room. If you want a meal look for **buffet de gare** or **bar-brasserie**. For a drink and snack go to a **buvette** or **bar**.

In some larger stations you can have showers (**douches**) or baths (**bains**).

There are facilities for changing money where you see **change** or **bureau de change**.
At many stations you can hire a car (**voiture** or **auto**). The sign will say **location de voitures** (car hire) or **service train + auto**.

cette this

This sign tells you that you can also hire a bicycle (**vélo**).

45

❓TEST YOURSELF

1 Identify these 'faux amis': **composter   quai**

2 You want to catch a train. Which is the railway station?

a
b
c

3 Which are the right signs if you want to (i) leave your luggage (ii) get information (iii) check train times (iv) buy a ticket (v) get something to eat (vi) sit and wait for the train?

a   b   c

d ✓   e

4 Which sign shows you the way to the subway?

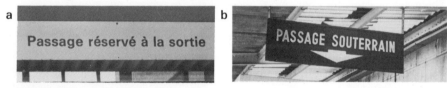

a
b

5 It's after midnight and you can't carry your luggage a step further. How do you solve your problem?

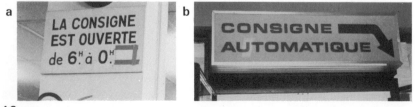

a
b

46

6 What is the gist of these signs?

a

composteur en dérangement

utiliser un autre appareil pour valider votre billet

b

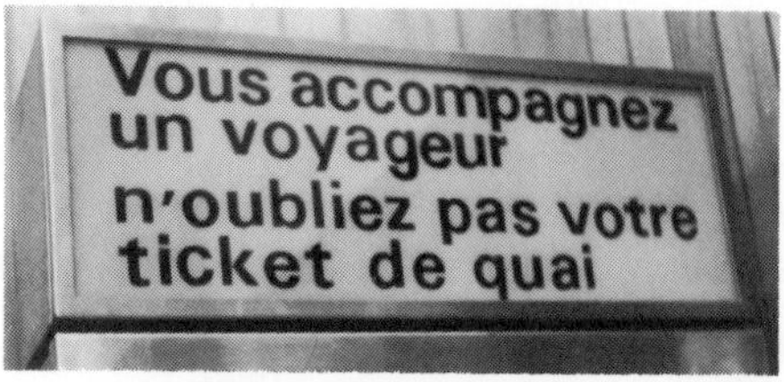

Vous accompagnez un voyageur n'oubliez pas votre ticket de quai

7 What's the difference between these two?

a

LOCATION DE VOITURES

b

POSITION DES VOITURES

8 What do these signs tell you?

a

VOITURES SANS CHAUFFEUR SERVICE **TRAIN +AUTO**

b

SERVICE TRAINS AUTOS - COUCHETTES →

c

TRAIN+VELO LOCATION au guichet **BAGAGES**

Innocent abroad:

ONE-MAN **CHARIOTS** FOR PASSENGERS? WHAT ABOUT THE KIDS?

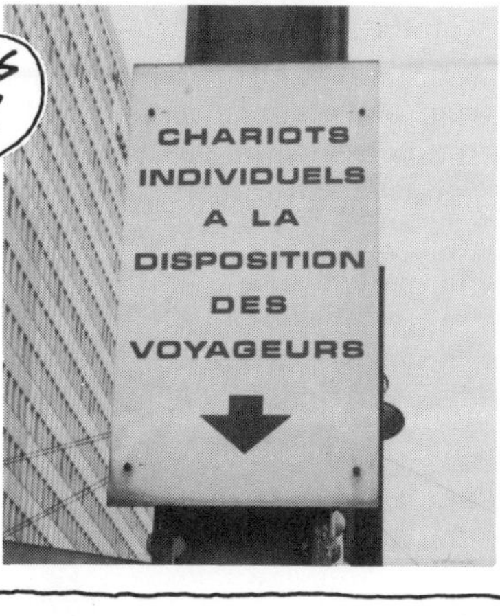

CHARIOTS INDIVIDUELS A LA DISPOSITION DES VOYAGEURS ↓

5 ACCOMMODATION

🔵 KEY WORDS

accueil
(welcome,
reception)

accueil de France (tourist office with room booking
service)
bureau d'accueil (reception)

chambre
(room)

chambre d'hôte (bed and breakfast)
chambre meublée (furnished room)
réservation de chambres (room booking service)

IMPORTANT WORDS

libre (vacant) **complet** (full)

Finding accommodation

If you want help with finding
somewhere to stay look for the official
tourist office **office de** (or **du**) **tourisme**
or **syndicat d'initiative**, or for **accueil de
France**.

Office
de
Tourisme

. . . a hotel or hostel

If you're looking for a hotel yourself,
watch out: some buildings called **hôtel**
are anything but hotels! You won't be
able to stay at the **hôtel de ville** (town
hall), **hôtel Dieu** (name of a hospital),
hôtel des ventes (auction rooms) or at
any of the old town houses known as
hôtel . . . (see p 62). A genuine hotel as
a rule has a sign **hôtel de tourisme**
giving its star rating.

Commissariat au tourisme
tourist board

This is sometimes followed by **NN**
(= **nouvelles normes**, new standards,
introduced some years ago).

Tout confort tells you it's a comfortable
hotel. Amenities advertised often include
bains (baths) and **douches** (showers).

HOTEL des ROSES

CHAMBRES TOUT CONFORT
BAINS-DOUCHES-W-C. PRIVÉS
Téléphone dans toutes les chambres

privés individual

If you want reasonable accommodation off the beaten track look for the sign **Logis de France**, an association of family-run hotels.

You can often get hotel accommodation in a **relais** (roadside inn) or **auberge** (inn) *but* **auberge jeunesse** or **auberge de jeunesse** is a youth hostel.

On the other hand **hostellerie** isn't a hostel or hostelry – it's a hotel.

. . a room

Private houses – and hotels – often advertise vacant rooms with **chambres à louer** (rooms to let), **chambres libres, chambres disponibles** or just **chambres**.

If you see **chambres d'hôte**, breakfast (**petit déjeuner**) is included in the price; **pension** means you'll be offered full board.
There's no point enquiring where you see this sign.

. . self-catering accommodation

If you want a furnished room look for **studio** (one-room flatlet *not* studio) or **chambre meublée**. Signs may also say **meublé touristique, hôtel meublé** (this doesn't mean you'll get hotel service!) or just **meublés** (furnished accommodation).

étage floor

You can often find furnished accommodation through an estate agent (**agent immobilier**). Adverts say **à louer** or **location** (letting).

In the countryside self-catering accommodation is known as a **gîte** (rural dwelling), but **gîtes** are so popular you'll be lucky to find a vacancy.

ruraux rural

Staying at a camp site

A camp site is called **camping**.

Charges are displayed at the entrance or the reception office (**bureau d'accueil**, **bureau** or **accueil**). Like hotels, camps have star rating (**étoiles**).

emplacent = **emplacement** pitch
moins 7 ans under 7

When you want to wash or shower make for **lavabos** (washbasins) or **douches**. Men look for **hommes**, women for **dames**.

toilette here personal hygiene *not* loo

A sink for washing crockery may be labelled **bac à** (or **de**) **vaisselle**, for clothing . . . **à linge**, for vegetables . . . **à légumes**.

But you mustn't wash where you see **défense de laver**.

To dispose of rubbish look for **poubelles** (dustbins).

eau potable drinking water

Notices with **feux de bois** (wood fires) and **barbecues** alert you to the fire risks (see p 95).

? TEST YOURSELF

1 Identify these 'faux amis': **hostellerie   location   pension   studio**

2 You're looking for somewhere to stay. Why could these signs be of interest?

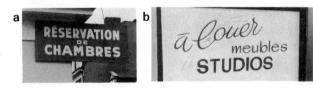

50

3 Which is the odd one out?

a   b   c

4 What are you being offered here?

a   b   c   d

5 You're looking for a camp site. Would this sign cheer you?

6 What do these camp site signs mean?

a   b   c

d

Innocent abroad:

DON'T FANCY THAT ONE. SOUNDS LIKE A CONVALESCENT HOME.

Hôtel des Invalides

6 AT THE POST OFFICE

🔵 KEY WORDS

courrier
(post, mail)

lettre
(letter)

boîte aux lettres (letterbox)

poste
(post office)

bureau de poste (post office)
poste centrale (main post office)
postes (postal service)
timbres-poste (postage stamps)

The French post office is known as **PTT**, short for **Postes, Télecommunications, Télédiffusion.**

On some post offices you can still see the older version **Poste, Télégraphe, Téléphone**. The post office colours are yellow and blue. Look for this symbol.

Opening hours

Most post offices are open morning and afternoon, but closed at lunchtime; to make certain, look for **heures d'ouverture** (opening hours) or **ouverture des guichets** (opening times of counters). Some main post offices are open throughout the day and provide a night service (**service de nuit**) for telegrams and telephones.

Buying stamps

At the post office look for the counter **timbres-poste** or **affranchissement**. Counters where stamps are sold only in small amounts say **timbres en détail**, if in large amounts **timbres en gros**.

Stamp collectors should look for **philatélie** or **timbres pour collections**.

Outside post offices you can get stamps from machines marked **timbres-poste**. If you haven't the right change (**monnaie**) look for a **changeur automatique** (coin-changing machine) (see chapter 7, p 57). Sometimes the two are combined into a **distributeur de timbres-poste et de monnaie**.

You can also get stamps from a tobacconist's (**tabac**) (see p 74, 83).

Posting a letter

Post boxes are marked **postes** or **boîte aux lettres**. They carry details of collection times (**heures des levées**). Some also tell you not to post large or bulky envelopes (**grosses lettres**), printed matter (**imprimés**), including newspapers (**journaux**).

tarif réduit reduced rate
jeter put
cette this
ni . . . ni neither . . . nor

Other letterboxes have separate slots for local mail (marked with the name of the area), for 'all other places' (**autres destinations**) and for different types of mail.

Letterboxes at post offices have frequent collections, but only state the time of the last collection (**dernière levée**).

(For days of the week see p 12.)

Inside the post office there's often a notice saying when the last post will leave: **le dernier départ du courrier est à . . .**

If you want to send a letter or parcel by registered mail you must take it to the counter labelled **objets recommandés** or **recommandation**.

Making a phone call

... from a public box

Phone boxes in the street are pale grey or beige. Only those that take 5F coins can be used for international as well as long-distance and local calls. The minimum charge is ½F; all calls are timed.

Phones for local calls only are sometimes marked **taxiphone** (they are *not* just for calling taxis!). You can often find one in a telephone 'shelter' (**abri**) at bus stops.

Instructions on these phones usually say **décrochez** (lift the receiver), **payez** (put the money in), **composez le numéro** (dial the number); when the subscriber answers you press a button.

... from the post office

There are coin-operated call boxes inside most post offices marked **cabine automatique**, **téléphone interurbain** (for calls inside France only) or **taxiphone**. For international calls you may have to go to the counter marked **téléphone** where you will be allocated a **cabine** (phone box); you pay at the counter when you've finished telephoning.

CABINE TÉLÉPHONIQUE

❷TEST YOURSELF

1 Identify these 'faux amis': **cabine   courrier**

2 You're in Nice and want to phone (i) your friends in Paris (ii) your family in Cardiff. Which phone would you ring from?

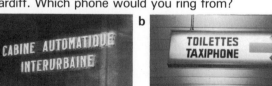

a   CABINE AUTOMATIQUE INTERURBAINE

b   TOILETTES TAXIPHONE

3 What should you post in the right hand slot?

LETTRES IMPRIMES

4 Which counter would be right if you wanted to

   (i) buy a few stamps for your postcards?

a

15 TIMBRES EN GROS
ET POUR COLLECTIONS
EXPRES AVION

b

17 AFFRANCHISSEMENTS DES
CORRESPONDANCES
OBJETS RECOMMANDES ET CHARGES

   (ii) register a letter

a

POSTE RESTANTE

TELEGRAPHE – TELEPHONE

EMISSION DES MANDATS

b

CHARGEMENT ET RECOMMANDATION

AFFRANCHISSEMENT

TIMBRES EN GROS

5 What information are you given here?

a

POSTES ET TELECOMMUNICATIONS
Nº 587

	OUVERTURE DES GUICHETS	LEVÉE DES BOITES DU BUREAU	
DU LUNDI AU VENDREDI	9H – 12H		
	14H – 17H	18H45	
LE SAMEDI	9H – 12H		
		14H45	

b

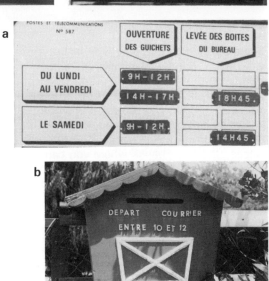

DEPART COURRIER
ENTRE 10 ET 12

7 COPING WITH MONEY

♀ KEY WORDS

billet
(note)

billet de banque (bank note)

caisse
(cash desk,
cashier's)

change
(exchange)

sometimes written **changes** – has to do with
changing money:
bureau de change (exchange bureau)
cours de changes (exchange rates)
changeur (machine for changing coins or notes)

monnaie
(small change,
coins)

changeur de monnaie (coin-changing machine)

pièce
(coin)

Where you can change money

At almost all banks.
You recognise them
by the word **banque**,
crédit, or **société**
(company).

Some banks are known by their initials
e.g. **BNP** = **Banque Nationale de Paris**.

Don't be misled by **Crédit Foncier**, that's
a finance company, or **Caisse d'Epargne**,
a savings bank: neither changes foreign
money.
Places other than banks where you can
change foreign cheques and currency
include airports, big railway stations and
exchange bureaux. Look for **change**,
bureau de change, devises (foreign
currency) – but *not* **échange de
monnaie**, that's a place where you can
get small change for parking fee and
other machines.

achat purchase
vente sale

Banking hours

Banks are normally open Mondays to Fridays, mornings and afternoons, and closed over lunch. But watch out for local variations. To check on opening hours look for **ouvert** (open), **ouverture** (opening time), **horaire** (times) coupled with **bureaux** (offices), **guichets** (counters) or **caisse**. (For days of the week see p 12.)

At airports and some railway stations you can also change money at weekends and often until late evening. Exchange bureaux are open during shopping hours.

To go into a bank you often have to ring (**sonner**) first. The bell may be marked **appel**.

attendre wait for **déclic** click
pousser push

Counters to look for in a bank

Watch out for **change** or **changes**, **étranger** (foreign counter) or **S^{ce}** (= service) **étranger**. But more often than not counters aren't labelled at all.

At the end of the transaction you generally collect your money from the cashier (**caisse**).

Coin-changing machines

For stamp, ticket, parking fee and other machines you may need small change (**monnaie**). Coin-changing machines are variously called **changeur automatique**, **changeur de monnaie**, **changeur pièces de monnaie**.

You insert the coin where it says **introduction**, **introduire**, **introduisez** or **mettez**; **rendu** (returned) tells you what change you'll get back.

Changeur de Monnaie		
Introduction:	5 F	1 F
Rendu:	5x1 F	1x ½ F
		2x20 cts
		1x 10 cts

Some machines will even change notes – **changeur billets de banque**. A machine that doesn't work may have a sticker saying **en panne** (broken down), **hors service** or **en dérangement** (out of order).

Coping with ticket and other machines

When you put coins into a ticket, parking fee or other machine, make sure it's the exact amount where it says **faites** (or **faire**) **l'appoint** – or where you're warned that the machine doesn't return change (**l'appareil ne rend pas la monnaie**).

doucement gently
une à une one by one

❓TEST YOURSELF

1 Identify these 'faux amis': **billet   change   crédit   monnaie   pièce**

2 It's half past 12 on Thursday. Can you change money at either of these places?

a   b

3 You want to cash some travellers' cheques. Which of these could you go to?

a   b   c   d   e

58

4 What will you get here?

5 (i) What do you have to do if you need small change for a stamp machine?

(ii) What do you have to do if you want to buy a train ticket from the machine?

Innocent abroad:

8 SIGHTSEEING

KEY WORDS

entrée (entrance, entry)	**droit d'entrée, prix d'entrée** (entrance fee) **entrée libre** (entry free of charge)
jour (day)	**journée** (whole day) **demi-journée** (half day) **journalier** (daily) (see also p 12)
tourisme (tourism)	**bureau de tourisme, office de tourisme** (tourist office) **grand tourisme** (luxury travel) **touristique** (of tourist interest, tourist . . .)
ville (town)	**centre ville** (town centre) **hôtel de ville** (town hall) **vieille ville, ville ancienne** (old part of the town)

To find out what there is to see

You can get brochures, maps etc. from the local tourist office. Look for **office de** (or **du**) **tourisme, syndicat d'initiative, accueil de France**, sometimes **bureau de tourisme**.

B^au^ = bureau

There's likely to be one in the town centre or at a big railway station (**gare**). Tourist information is also available where you see 🛈 or **renseignements touristiques**
but **services de tourisme** usually refers to transport services laid on for tourists (see top of next page).

If you travel by car, watch as you approach a town for signs listing its attractions. They often start with **visitez** or **touristes, arrêtez-vous** (stop).

You sometimes see brown and white signs along the route; they alert you to places of interest.

Taking a trip

For an organised sightseeing tour (**excursion**) go to an **agence de voyage** (travel agency) or enquire where you see **services de tourisme** or **ST**, often at a station. Many trips are run by French Railways (**SNCF**) in coaches (**autocars**) or boats (**bateaux**) as well as trains.

To find the time or place of departure look for **départ** or the time in figures, for the time of return **retour**. Fares may be given just in figures or under **tarifs**, **prix** (prices) or **prix des places** (seat prices); **aller-retour** means you can get a return ticket.

You buy your ticket where it says **billets** (tickets), **vente de billets** or **vente de tickets** (sale of tickets).

mont mount

Sightseeing in town

A sightseeing tour is a **visite**. If you want to explore the town centre for yourself follow the sign **centre ville**. To visit the old part of a town look for **ville ancienne**, **vieille ville**, **cité** or **vieux quartier** (old quarter).

chaque soir every evening

In old towns it may be worth looking for signs with **remparts** (town walls) or **tour** (tower — beware: **tour** sometimes means 'trip'). Other attractions are mentioned on signs headed **monuments historiques et sites** (historic buildings and places) or **sites et curiosités** (places of interest).

pont suspendu suspension bridge

You can often tell when a place was built by looking for a Roman numeral with **e** or **ième** followed by **s** for **siècle**, (century).

églises churches **point de vue** viewing point

Guided tours

They are called **visites guidées** or **accompagnées**. You're asked (**prié**) to wait for (**attendre**) the guide at a certain spot.

For independent sightseeing you can sometimes hire a cassette commentary.

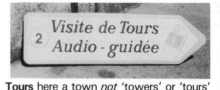

Tours here a town *not* 'towers' or 'tours'

Looking at churches . . .

Churches of special interest are often signposted. Look for **église, cathédrale, abbaye** (abbey), **chapelle** and **basilique** (basilica).

Sacré-Coeur Sacred Heart

. . . castles and palaces

You can't go far without seeing signs to **château**. This may be anything from a fortified or moated castle to a palace (like Versailles) or a spacious country house.

Palais can be a palace (like Fontainebleau) or an important public building like **palais de justice** (law courts)

but **palais** can also be the name for a large hall — **palais des congrès** (congress hall), **palais des festivals** (festival hall), and it's fashionable to call blocks of luxury flats **palais.**

Elegant old buildings called **hôtel** may be worth a visit — they're not hotels but old town houses or the **hôtel de ville** itself.

. . . museums and exhibitions

The name of a museum often tells you what to expect — **musée des beaux arts** (fine arts), **histoire locale, coiffes d'Anjou** (headdresses from Anjou).

But it's frequently just the name of the building (**musée du Louvre**) or perhaps of the town or region (**musée de Normandie**).

folklore local customs

Inside museums there may be reminders not to smoke (**fumer**) or to touch or photograph objects.

tapisseries tapestries

A sign with **suite** or **sens** (direction) tells you which way to go.

If you want to see a special exhibition within a museum or elsewhere look for **exposition** or **expo** for short.

en permanence permanently open
peinture paintings

. . . parks, gardens and zoos

Look for **parc** (park) and **jardin** (garden). Castle grounds are usually called **jardins**. **Jardin zoologique** or **jardin d'acclimatation** is a zoo; **jardin des plantes** means botanical gardens *but* **jardin d'été** (**été** = summer) generally turns out to be a garden outside a restaurant, **jardin d'enfants** is a kindergarten, and **parc autos** or **parc de stationnement** is a car park.

In most parks and gardens you're requested to keep off the lawns (**pelouses**).

Times when places are open

Look for **ouvert**, **heures d'ouverture** or **horaire d'ouverture** (opening hours) or just a list of the days and times when places are open. Many museums and castles close on Monday or Tuesday; nearly all of them close for lunch.

matin morning   **pièces meublées** furnished rooms

Getting a ticket

The ticket office may be marked **billets, tickets** or **guichet** (counter). **Entrée, prix d'entrée, droit d'entrée, tarif** all mean entrance fee. Reduced rates (**tarif réduit** or **demi-tarif**) usually apply to **étudiants** (students), **scolaires** (school children), **enfants** (children), **groupes** and **familles nombreuses** (large families).

When visits are free you'll see **gratuit** or **entrée libre**. Children under a certain age (**moins de . . . ans**) don't pay, but age limits vary.

Exploring the countryside

Tourist routes of scenic, historic or other interest are marked **route** or **Rte.**, e.g. **route des crêtes** (ridgeway road), **route du vin** (route through wine-growing areas), **route pittoresque** (scenic route).

One that brings you back to your starting point is called **circuit**.

Signs with **lac** (lake), **vallée** (valley), **grotte** or **caverne** (cave) − but *not* **cave** (see next paragraph) − often take you to places of scenic interest.

If you want to go up a mountain the easy way there may be a cable railway (**téléphérique**).

Sampling the local wine

In many regions of France you're invited to visit a wine cellar (**cave** or **caveau**) and sample (**déguster**) the local vintage.

If the local wines are at all special it may say so on signs at the edge of towns, e.g. **grands vins** (great wines), **vins renommés** (renowned wines), **appellation contrôlée** (guaranteed quality).

Posters with **foire aux vins** (**foire** = fair) are advertising wine festivals, often with **dégustation gratuite** (free wine-tasting)!

col pass

cygnes swans

roc rock

ses primeurs its early vegetables

TEST YOURSELF

1 Identify these 'faux amis': **circuit   cité   curiosités   exposition   hôtel   monument   palais   tour**

2 All these signs point to tourist attractions. What are they?

a   Centre Vieille Ville

b   CAVE TOURISTIQUE

c   ACCES AUX JARDINS

d   LES CHATELLIERS
BEAU PANORAMA SUR
LA VILLE ET LA LOIRE

e   *Circuit Touristique*

3 You've just arrived by train and would like some brochures about the town before you explore. Can any of these places help?

a   OFFICE DE TOURISME
ACCUEIL DE FRANCE

b   *Syndicat d'Initiative*

c   **AUTOCARS**   SERVICES
VOYAGES - EXCURSIONS   REGULIERS

4 You're a culture vulture. Which of these would you include in a sightseeing trip?

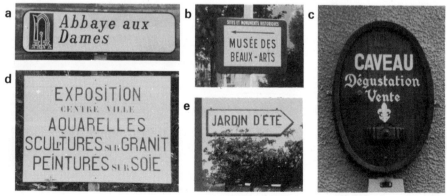

a   *Abbaye aux Dames*

b   SITES ET MONUMENTS HISTORIQUES
MUSÉE DES BEAUX - ARTS

c   CAVEAU
Dégustation
Vente

d   EXPOSITION
CENTRE VILLE
AQUARELLES
SCULTURES sur GRANIT
PEINTURES sur SOIE

e   JARDIN D'ÉTÉ

5 You want to explore the neighbourhood. What are the options?

a ROUTE DU CIDRE

b visitez **LAON** ses remparts, ses abbayes sa chapelle des Templiers son musée

c Parc de Bel Air Jardin Public

6 Your friends like looking at old buildings and works of art — you prefer to be outdoors. Which offers the best compromise?

a TOUR DU LAC

b VISITES DE LA VILLE ANCIENNE ET DU CHATEAU 10h50 • 15h • 17h SYNDICAT D'INITIATIVE OFFICE DU TOURISME DÉPART A 60M

c Visitez les GROTTES PETRIFIANTES de SAVONNIÈRES

7 On what days are these places open?

a Veuve Amiot
visite des caves
jours ouvrables   9 à 11.30
                         15 à 16.30
samedis, dimanches   10 à 11.30
et jours fériés   15 à 17.30
              d'avril a Septembre

b MUSÉE SAINT JEAN
TOUS LES JOURS
DE 10h. A 12h.
DE 14h. A 18h.
PRIX D'ENTRÉE = 2f.

8 You want to visit the castle with your children aged 12 and 15.
(i) What does it say about children?
(ii) When does half-price apply?
(iii) Is it open on Sunday mornings?

LE CHATEAU EST OUVERT
TOUS LES JOURS
de 9h à 18h45
DROIT d'ENTREE : tarif . 6F
DIMANCHES et FETES , demi-tarif .3F
INTERDIT AUX ENFANTS DE MOINS
DE 13 ANS NON ACCOMPAGNÉS .
INTERDIT AUX ANIMAUX .

Innocent abroad:

ANY **STALACTITES** IN THERE, I WONDER ?

VISITES DES CAVES

9 OUT IN THE OPEN

Cycling (See also chapter 2)

KEY WORDS

cycles (bicycles)	**bicyclette** (bicycle)
	cyclable, cycliste (for cyclists)
	but **cyclos** are motorised bicycles
vélos (bicycles)	the most commonly used word for 'bikes'
2 roues (two-wheelers)	

Hiring a bike

You can hire cycles in many places, including larger railway stations. Look for **location** (hire) **de vélos, location 2 roues, vélos à louer** (for hire), or at a station **ici train + vélo**.

Cycling around

Alongside a few roads is a cycle track (**piste cyclable**) which you should use. In some holiday areas there may be a signposted cycle ride — **itinéraire cycliste recommandé**.

You can often go where other vehicles are prohibited — look for **sauf** . . . but there are a number of places where you may not ride a bike (**circuler à bicyclette**).

circulation traffic
stationnement parking

Parking' your bike

There are often special places to leave bikes, e.g. **parc à vélos, garage de vélos, P 2 roues**.

There are even more places where you shouldn't 'park' a bike, e.g. on the pavement (**sur le trottoir**), or at some 'no waiting' signs.

You may be told not to leave (**déposer**) or lean (**appuyer**) it somewhere.

Walking

🙂 KEY WORDS

pédestre	**promenade pédestre** (walk)
(on foot)	**tourisme pédestre** (hiking)

How to discover good walks

If you're just out for a stroll look for **promenade pédestre, circuit pédestre** (path round a particular area), or **petite randonnée** (short ramble).

pittoresque picturesque

Keen walkers look for **tourisme pédestre, sentier** (footpath) **de . . .** or **grande randonnée** (long ramble) or just **GR**. Each route has a coloured symbol and many are numbered.

Finding out how far your destination is

Signposts give distances in hours (**h = heures**) and minutes, rarely in kilometres.

ferme farm   **vallée** valley

They sometimes tell you where food and shelter are available. For accommodation look for **refuge** (shelter), **gîte d'étape** (overnight halt), **hébergement** (lodging); for accommodation and food watch out for **ferme** or **ferme auberge** (**auberge** = inn).

Trois Fours Three Ovens (name of inn)

Going swimming

KEY WORDS

se baigner
(to bathe)

baignade (bathing)
baigneurs (bathers)

bains
(bathing)

but **bains municipaux, bains-douches** indicate where
people can go for a bath or shower, not a swim; you also
see **bains** in names of spas e.g. **Aix-les-Bains**.

Bathing in the sea, lakes, rivers

Make for **plage** (beach) or **baignade**.

Baignade surveillée (supervised) tells you
that life-guards are on duty. Don't bathe where
you see **bains interdits** or **baignade interdite**.
On Mediterranean beaches you sometimes have
to pay, but not where it says **plage publique** or
plage en régie municipale (municipal beach).

Going to a swimming pool

Look for **piscine**. There's usually one in a
sports centre (**complexe sportif, palais
des sports** or **parc des sports**).

Piscine chauffée or **climatisée** tells you
it's a heated pool. Big sports centres
may have more than one swimming pool
(**bassin**), and perhaps even a paddling
pool (**patangeoire**).

Paying to go in

The list of charges is usually headed **tarif**
or **prix** (prices). There may be cheap
rates e.g. for children (**enfants**), students
(**étudiants**); look for **tarif réduit** (reduced
price) or **demi-tarif** (half price) though it
may not be exactly half the full price
(**plein tarif**)!

carnet book

Getting changed

Communal changing rooms are
vestiaires, individual cubicles are
cabines. The section for men is marked
messieurs, the one for women **dames**.

Boating

Taking a boat

If you want to go boating look for **bateaux** (boats) or the names of different types of boat: **barques** are rowing boats, **pédalos** are pedal boats, for the lazy there may be **canots à moteur** (motor boats), for sailing enthusiasts **bateaux à voile** or **voiliers** *but* **planches à voile** are sailboards.

Prices are usually quoted per half hour (**demi-heure**).

Going on an organised boat trip

Look for **vedette** or **bateau mouche** (motor launch) or just **bateaux**.

By the seaside you may also see **promenades** or **sorties en mer** (trips out to sea); by a lake it may say **tour du lac**.

Port de plaisance directs you to the yacht harbour or marina; **embarcadères** to the landing stages *but* **embarcations** means small boats.

promenades trips

golfe bay   billets tickets
renseignements information

Somewhere for the children to play

enfants (children)	**garderie d'enfants** (nursery)
jeux (games)	**jeux de ballon** (ball games)
	parc de jeux (playground)

There are often places where children can play. Look for **parc de jeux** and **jeux pour enfants** *but* **jeu de boules** indicates a place for Frenchmen to play bowls.

direction management

Elsewhere you'll come across many signs forbidding ball games.

1 Identify these 'faux amis': **ballon   embarcation   location   promenade**

2 You'd like an after-dinner stroll. Which route looks best?

a

b

c

3 You want to hire a bike. Which of these signs can help?

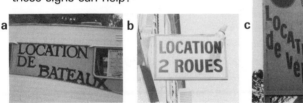

a   b   c

4 If you're cycling what do these signs tell you?

a   b   c

71

5 At which of these places can you swim?

a PLAGE PUBLIQUE *Régie Municipale*

b PISCINE MUNICIPALE DE L'ECCE HOMO

c BAIGNADE INTERDITE

6 The lake looks inviting. What are the possibilities?

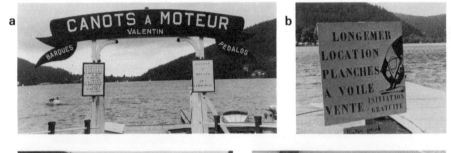

a CANOTS A MOTEUR VALENTIN BARQUES PEDALOS

b LONGEMER LOCATION PLANCHES A VOILE VENTE INITIATION GRATUITE

c ICI DEPART VEDETTE TOUR DU LAC

d il est formellement interdit de se baigner depuis les embarcations

7 You've two young children with you. What do these signs tell you?

a jeux de ballon interdits dans le square

b GARDERIE D'ENFANTS PARC DE JEUX GRATUITS

c JEU de Boules

Innocent abroad:

GOLF ON THE BEACH? MUST BE ONE HUGE BUNKER!

GOLF DE LONGEMER JEUX DE PLAGE LOCATION CABINE/ SIEGE/ PARASOL/ BOISSON/ A EMPORTER CONFISERIE · GLACES/

10 SHOPS AND SERVICES

KEY WORDS

achat
(purchase)

caisse   **ticket de caisse** (receipt)
(cash desk,
checkout)

magasin
(shop)

maison   often indicates a specialist shop:
(house,   **maison de la presse** (name of book-cum-newspaper
home-made)   shop)

marché   **hypermarché** (hypermarket)
(market)   **supermarché** (supermarket)
                              marchandise (goods)

prix
(price)

soldes   **derniers soldes** (end-of-sale)
(sales)   **soldes été** (summer sale)

vente   **après-vente** (after-sale service)
(sale)

Shop signs to look for

Most shops advertise their goods and services more prominently than the
name of the shop. Look for words with . . . **erie**
  cordonnerie (shoemaker's)
  mercerie (haberdashery)
  maroquinerie (leather goods)
  papeterie (stationer's)
but there are some misleading names
  librairie (bookshop *not* a library —
  that's **bibliothèque**)
  droguerie (sells household articles,
  toiletries etc. *not* drugs)
  bonneterie (sells underwear, baby
  clothes etc. *not* bonnets).

confection clothes
nettoyage cleaning

Or look for what you want to buy
chaussures (shoes), **journaux** (newspapers),
livres (books), **prêt-à-porter** (ready-to-wear
fashions), **tabac(s)** (cigarettes, tobacco, but
also newspapers, stamps, postcards).

Libre service tells you it's self-service,
but **entrée libre** invites you to look
round.

If you want souvenirs or presents

Look for **souvenirs** and **cadeaux**
(presents). If you're invited to someone's
home the custom is to buy flowers
(**fleurs**) for your hostess.

Spotting a bargain

Any mention of **prix** should attract you: **prix réduits** (reduced prices), **prix
refroidis** (no price increases – **refroidis** = frozen), **prix chocs** (amazing
prices – **choc** = shock), **prix vacances** (holiday prices).

Reductions are described as **réduction** or
remise, a special offer as **promotion**,
promo or **réclame**, outstanding value as
performance and this week's offer as
affaire de la semaine (**semaine** = week).

costumes suits

Soldes tells you that there's a sale on,
not that the goods are already sold!

Look out also for **moins cher** (cheaper).

Shopping in department stores

Some popular stores include **prix** (or **pris**)
or **galeries** in their names, e.g. **Prisunic,
Monoprix, Nouvelles Galeries**. The
different departments carry signs similar
to the ones you see on shops
(**chaussures, droguerie, parfumerie**) or
they say what the goods are for; some
end in . . . **age** e.g. **jardin** or **jardinage**
(gardening), **bricolage** (DIY), **ménage**
(household).

à l'intérieur inside

la cuisine
le jardin
le bricolage
la droguerie

cuisine kitchen

74

Normally you pay where it says **caisse**.
You may be asked to keep (**conservez**)
your receipt.

vos your

You may also see reminders to pay
(**réglez**).

rayon
department
confiserie
confectionery

Supermarket and hypermarket shopping

Household articles as well as food are sold
in some supermarkets (**supermarchés**)
and in vast hypermarkets (**hypermarchés**)
on the edge of towns. The various
sections are clearly labelled e.g.
surgelé(s) (frozen food), **vaisselle**
(crockery), **lessives** (soaps and washing
powders).

At the entrance you'll see notices asking
you to use a trolley (**caddie** or **chariot**) or
a basket (**panier**).

At the checkout you may be asked to
open (**ouvrir**) your shopping bags (**sacs**
or **cabas**). If you haven't bought anything
leave where it says **sortie sans achat**.

prenez take

Food shopping

Besides supermarkets or hypermarkets many stores have a self-service food
department (**alimentation**), usually in the basement (**sous-sol**). Or you can go to
an open air market (**marché**) or a covered one (**halles**) — they're held most
mornings, including Sundays.

There are also plenty of small food shops:

* for bread look for **boulangerie**
  (baker's); if the shop sign says
  boulangerie pâtisserie they also sell
  pastries and cakes

* for fresh fruit look for **fruits**, for
  vegetables **légumes** though it often
  says **primeurs** (early vegetables)
  instead

chez at

75

* for a shop that sells groceries and greengroceries it will say **comestibles**, **alimentation** or **alimentation générale**

* for groceries look too, for **épicerie**; **épicerie fine** means they sell select, more expensive groceries

* for prepared dishes and delicatessen find a **traiteur** or a shop advertising **plats cuisinés** (ready-cooked food)

* for fresh meat go to a **boucherie**; if the sign also says **charcuterie** they sell cooked meats as well *but* **boucherie chevaline** or just **chevaline** means it's a horse butcher's (**cheval** = horse)

* for poultry (**volailles**) you can go to a **boucherie**, a fish shop (**poissonnerie**) or a dairy (**crèmerie**)

* for dairy produce, besides **crèmerie**, look for **fromagerie** (cheese shop), **fromage** (cheese), **beurre** (butter), **oeufs** (eggs), **lait** (milk). Milk (which isn't delivered to homes) comes in cartons or plastic bottles marked **frais** (fresh) or **longue conservation** (long-life).

autre pavillon other building
gibiers game

* for wine and spirits look for **vins** (wines), **vins spiritueux** (spirits), **liqueurs**, or **cave(s)** (wine cellar *not* a cave).

bons good

Finding out what you get for your money

Fresh foods are priced and sold
* by the kilogram: look for **kilo** or **kg**
* by the pound (i.e. 500 grams): **la livre**, ½ **kilo** or ½ **kg**
  (Note: English pound = 454 g.)
* singly: **la pièce** (each)
* by the dozen: **la douzaine** or **douz.**

Fresh foods are graded. For top quality look for:
c I, cl.I (class I),
1ère cat. (1st category),
1er choix (1st choice).

Locally grown or produced food is described as **pays** or **du pays**.

Home-made food is called . . . **maison** e.g. **pâté maison**, home-made pâté.

fraise strawberries

Things you may be asked to do . . .

Servez-vous (serve yourself), **prenez un sac** (take a bag), **faites peser** (have it weighed).

. . and not to do

Ne pas toucher à la marchandise (don't touch goods), **ne pas se servir** (don't serve yourself).

Getting things done . . .

If you need to have something repaired, watch out for **réparations** (repairs).

For shoe repairs you can also go to a **cordonnerie** or where you see a sign **talons minute** (while-you-wait heel bar — **talons** = heels, **minute** = the time you have to wait!).

clés keys

If you want to go to the hairdresser, find a **coiffeur, salon** or **coiffure**. Ladies look for **dames**, men for **messieurs, hommes** or **masculine**. (**Masculine** means 'for men', not a male hairdresser.)

. . . or cleaned

Launderettes are few and far between. The sign will say **laverie** or **lavomatique**.
If you can't find a launderette and want something washed or cleaned look for **blanchisserie** (laundry) or **nettoyage à sec** (dry-cleaning). A price list is usually displayed in the window or on the outside of the shop.

jumpers	
skirts	
trousers	
jackets	
dresses	

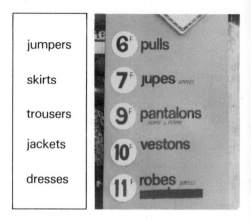

Shopping hours

Signs headed **ouvert** or **horaires d'ouverture** give details of opening times. Most shops take a long lunch break but stay open quite late – 7 or 7.30 pm. Those that stay open all day sometimes advertise this with **journées continues** or **sans interruption**. For late-night shopping look for **nocturne**.

Most shops close one day a week. It may say **fermé le . . .** or **fermeture hebdomadaire** (weekly closing) or **ouvert tous les jours sauf . . .** (open every day except . . .).

Food shops are often open on Sunday mornings but rarely on a Monday.
In summer you'll find some shops closed for annual holidays (**congés**). There'll be a notice saying **fermeture annuelle** or **fermé pour congés**.

août August   inclus inclusive

❓TEST YOURSELF

1 The shopping scene is riddled with 'faux amis'. Try to identify these:
affaire cave costumes droguerie librairie promotion rayon soldes

2 Which sign is right if you want to

(i) buy pork chops?

(ii) get food and knives and forks?

a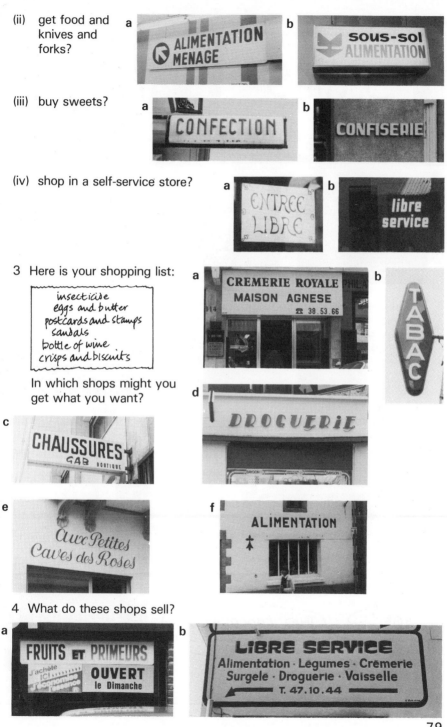
ALIMENTATION MENAGE

b
sous-sol ALIMENTATION

(iii) buy sweets?

a
CONFECTION

b
CONFISERIE

(iv) shop in a self-service store?

a
ENTREE LIBRE

b
libre service

3 Here is your shopping list:

> insecticide
> eggs and butter
> postcards and stamps
> sandals
> bottle of wine
> crisps and biscuits

In which shops might you get what you want?

a
CREMERIE ROYALE PHILA
MAISON AGNESE
☎ 38.53.66

b
TABAC

c
CHAUSSURES
GAB BOUTIQUE

d
DROGUERIE

e
Aux Petites
Caves des Roses

f
ALIMENTATION

4 What do these shops sell?

a
FRUITS ET PRIMEURS
J'achète ICI
OUVERT
le Dimanche

b
LIBRE SERVICE
Alimentation · Légumes · Crèmerie
Surgelé · Droguerie · Vaisselle
T. 47.10.44

79

5 What would make you stop here?

a
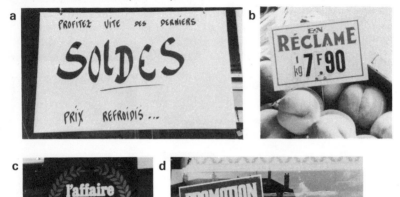

PROFITEZ VITE DES DERNIERS

SOLDES

PRIX REFROIDIS ...

b

EN RÉCLAME
1 kg 7F.90

c

l'affaire de la semaine

d

PROMOTION

VENTE EXCEPTIONNELLE

6 You're in a store. What do these signs mean?

a sortie sans achat interdite

b caisse caisse →

c avant de quitter le sous-sol réglez vos achats

7 Which is the right place to go to if (i) you want to buy a blouse (ii) want a pair of shoes heeled (iii) your hair needs cutting?

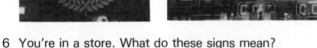

a CORDONNERIE TALON MINUTE MODERNE SAUVEUR Fils

b SALON DAMES

c Marie Christine PRET A PORTER

Innocent abroad:

THAT CHOCOLATE IS A BIT PRICEY!

OPÉRATION VACANCES 50 Prix Choc

11 EATING OUT AND DRINKING

▶KEY WORDS

déjeuner (lunch)	**petit déjeuner** (breakfast)
frit (fried)	**friterie** (stall or shop sellling freshly fried food including chips) **frites** or **pommes frites**, short for **pommes de terre frites** (chips) **friture** (mixed fried fish)
glace (ice)	**glaces** (ice-creams) **glacier** (ice-cream parlour)
plat (dish)	**plat à emporter** (take-away food) **plat du jour** (today's special) **plats cuisinés** (ready-cooked food)

f you want a meal

The two main meals of the day are **déjeuner**, served from about noon till 2.30 pm and **dîner** from about 7 pm onwards.

Most eating places just display their names or advertise their specialities, e.g. **grillades** (grills), **fruits de mer** (sea food), **poissons** (fish).

goûter afternoon tea
souper late supper

bouillabaisse provençal fish soup
langouste variety of lobster

When you see the word **restaurant** it may merely mean that hot food is available; for instance, **bar restaurant** is a place where you can get food as well as drinks. For a family-type restaurant, often in rural areas, look for **auberge** (inn). Many of them advertise regional specialities or local ones, described as **du pays** (of the country), e.g. **vin du pays** (local wine).

81

If you don't have time for a leisurely meal a **brasserie** may be the answer: they serve a selection of simple hot dishes that can be prepared in a few minutes such as **steack grillé frites** (grilled steak with chips), **brochettes** (skewered meat).

On main roads you often come across roadside inns called **relais**. They provide substantial inexpensive meals, sometimes set meals only.

VRP = **voyageurs représentants placiers** commercial travellers

Some belong to the network of transport drivers' restaurants with the symbol **les routiers** (**route** = road).

At railway stations look for **buffet** or **buffet de gare**. You can also get a meal — though the choice may not be great — at a **café** or a place called **snack**. If you'd like to try the savoury and sweet pancakes (**crêpes**) typical of Brittany go to a **crêperie**.

If you're looking for that typical French **bistro** (or **bistrot**), be warned: there are not as many of them around as you may think.

Self-service

Look for **cafétéria**, **self** or **libre service** (self-service).

Snacks

Apart from most self-service restaurants, places advertising **casse-croûte** provide hot and cold snacks. So do most **cafés**, **bars** and a number of other eating places; **à toute heure** tells you that food is available at any time.

A popular snack is **croque monsieur** (toasted double decker sandwich with ham and cheese); with an egg on top it's called **croque madame**.

82

Many outdoor stalls also offer snacks. Besides **sandwichs** typical snacks are **frites**, often sold at a **friterie**, **saucisses** (sausages), **merguez** (spicy barbecued sausages) and **crêpes**.

Cakes and pastries

The best place for these is a **salon de thé** (tea room) often attached to a **pâtisserie** (cake shop). There you get cakes and pastries, usually made on the premises, as well as drinks including tea.

Ices

If you're keen on ice-cream watch out for **glaces**. They are sold in some food-shops and small restaurants, from stalls and vending machines, but above all at a **glacier** (ice-cream parlour); **maison** (home, house) tells you that they're home-made, **à emporter** or **portatives** that they're for taking away; **sorbet** is a water-ice, and **parfum** means flavour (*not* perfume)

but **glace à rafraîchir** is ice for cooling.

fraise strawberry   **citron** lemon   **simple** single

Drinks

An obvious place for a drink is a **bar**. They serve alcoholic and soft drinks including coffee from early morning till late at night. Most of them also provide breakfast (**petit déjeuner**), snacks and often meals. Many sell cigarettes and tobacco – and stamps; the sign will say **bar tabac** or **bar tabacs**. Some even sell newspapers (**journaux**).

PMU (= **Pari Mutuel Urbain**) in letters often bigger than the name of the bar merely means that you can place a bet (**pari**) there.

You can get cold drinks, beer etc. from a stall marked **buvette** (refreshment bar)

or from one that advertises **boissons** (drinks, *not* **poissons**, that's fish!). If you see **boissons fraîches** it means chilled (*not* fresh) drinks.

pan bagnat large filled roll
(provençal speciality)

Especially in wine-growing areas you'll come across signs with **dégustation** inviting you to sample the local wine. Look for **dégustation gratuite** (free sampling) or **dégustation ici** *but* **dégustation de fruits de mer** tells you that a restaurant provides choice sea food.

For a glass of beer (**bière**) the best place is often a **brasserie**. If you want draught beer watch out for **pression** or **à la pression**.

Ready-cooked food

There is a great variety, from salads and savouries to **poulet rôti** (roast chicken). Sometimes you can even buy a full meal, hot or intended for reheating. Look for **charcuterie** if you want ham (**jambon**), pâtés, sliced meats and salads, **traiteur** (caterer) or **plats cuisinés** for a wider selection of prepared dishes.

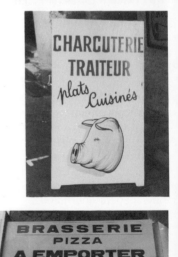

For take-away food it will say **à emporter**.

Menus

Practically every eating place provides a **menu** (fixed price meal), usually three courses with a limited choice of dishes. In holiday resorts there is often a lower priced **menu touristique** or a special **menu vacances** (**vacances** = holidays)
but if you want the menu with a free choice of dishes look for **carte** or **carte du jour** (today's menu).

Most restaurants offer a **plat du jour** ('today's special').

à huile in oil
assiette charcuterie mixed cold meats
nature plain

It's worth finding out if service is included (**service compris**) or if the price includes wine or other drinks (**vin compris, boisson comprise**).

repas meal

Opening hours

There are no licensing hours, so restaurants, cafés, and bars can stay open till late at night. Beware: most restaurants and ready-cooked food shops close one day each week. The sign at the door will say **fermé** plus the day of the week.

Sometimes there is a notice saying when they are open (**ouvert**).

85

❷ TEST YOURSELF

1 Identify these 'faux amis': **carte fraîche glacier menu parfum plat poisson**

2 When would you welcome this sign?

3 You can get a hamburger or a hot dog (**le vrai** − 'the real one') here. What else?

4 What kind of eating places are these?

a
b
c

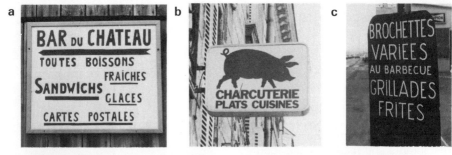

5 What sort of food or drink would you get here?

a
b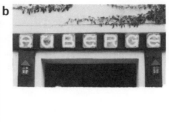
c

d
e

86

6 These bars are more than just bars — why?

7 Where could you be sure of getting take-away ices?

Innocent abroad:

12 LOOKING FOR A LOO

IMPORTANT WORDS   **libre** (vacant)
    occupé (engaged)
    hors service
      (out of order)

Names for loos

The usual description is **WC** or
toilette(s). You may also see **sanitaires** –
particularly on motorway lay-bys – but
many loos are not identified.

Women look for **dames** or **femmes**,
men for **messieurs** or **hommes**, but
you may have to go inside the
main door before you see either.
For men there are also **urinoirs**
(urinals). You may also come
across **elle** (she) and **lui** (he).

But beware **privé** – it just means 'private'!

In eating places and bars you generally
find loos next to the telephone.

What it costs

The usual thing is to give a tip, 50 **centimes**
or 1 **franc**, to the woman attendant who
services the 'ladies' as well as the 'gents' and
sometimes sits between the entrances to
both. In public loos she may also sell the loo
paper.

Slot machines to operate loo doors
are not very common. Where they
do exist you may need a ½ **franc**
coin (= 50 **centimes**) or coins to
the value of 1 franc, for instance
for the Parisian superloos
(**sanisettes**).

toilettes

Pour entrer,
mettez 1 franc
en pièces de :
10c - 20c - 50c ou 1F.
La porte s'ouvre et se ferme
comme une porte normale.

> to go in
> insert 1 franc
> in 10c 20c 50c or 1F coins
> the door opens and closes like
> a normal door

Other facilities

In some loos the attendant will look after (**garder**) your parcels (**colis**) – and in Paris especially men can get their shoes cleaned if it says **cireur**.

Others, including main line station loos (often run by commercial firms like **Relais**), also offer washing and showering facilities. Look for **douche** (shower), **cabinet** or **cab. de toilette** (cubicle with WC, wash basin, and in the 'ladies', bidet; **toilette** here means 'wash and brush up').

TEST YOURSELF

1 If you can't find a sign **dames** which of these might be the right one?

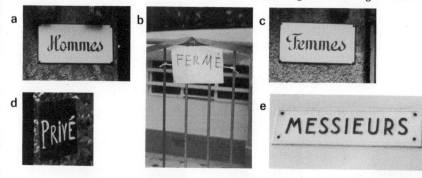

2 What information do these signs provide?

(if this sign puzzles you check with chapter 11)

Don't be taken in – **toilettage** is a dog parlour.

13 IF YOU FEEL ILL

🔵 KEY WORDS

urgence
(emergency)

service d'urgence (emergency service)
soins d'urgence, urgences (emergency treatment, casualty department)

If you need medicine or a simple remedy

Look for **pharmacie** (dispensing chemist's) or the (green) emblem you see outside this chemist's shop.

Every **pharmacie** sells proprietary drugs and medicines, ointments, bandages etc. and dispenses doctors' prescriptions (**ordonnances**); some sell a limited range of toiletries and cosmetics. Most chemists offer advice for common ailments and can give first aid for cuts, stings etc.

When the chemist's is closed, the notice **service de garde**, **service d'urgence** or **pharmacie de service** will tell you which chemist is open.

assuré undertaken

Don't be misled by **droguerie** — they don't sell drugs, but household articles, hardware, toiletries, etc.

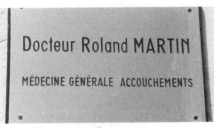

accouchements confinements

If you need a doctor

If you see a sign with **docteur** on it, it doesn't follow that you've found a doctor of medicine — some dentists, for example, call themselves **docteur** or **Dr**. If you want a GP look for **médecine générale** below the name; some GPs also specialise in a particular branch of medicine.

Occasional signs directing you to a doctor's surgery say **médecin** *not* **docteur**.

infirmière nurse

If you have a toothache

You need to find a **chirurgien-dentiste** (dental surgeon). As a rule they will see you by appointment (**sur rendez-vous**) only. Other information on a sign may mean that the dentist is a specialist and won't normally treat toothache.

If the sign mentions **urgences** you can have emergency treatment.

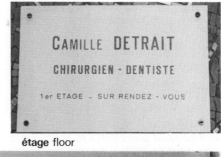

étage floor

Surgery hours

Some doctor's signs list surgery hours. Look for **consultations**. (For days of the week see p 12.)

If you have to go to hospital

Follow the sign **H** (for **hôpital**) or **centre hospitalier**, sometimes shortened to **CH**, or **CHU** if it's a teaching hospital (**U** = **universitaire**).

Clinique is often a private fee-paying clinic. Don't be misled by **hôtel Dieu** – it's neither a hotel nor a place of worship (**Dieu** = God), but in some towns it's the main hospital.

At the hospital make for **urgences** or **soins d'urgence**.

To call an ambulance see p 94.

❓TEST YOURSELF

1 Identify these 'faux amis': **hôtel Dieu   médecin   urgence**

2 You have toothache. Who is the right person to see?

3 When can you see (i) this dentist   (ii) this doctor?

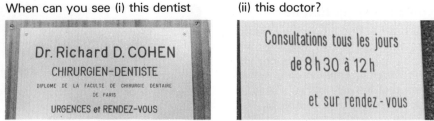

4 You need something to soothe a cough. Which sign should you follow for a quick remedy?

5 Your friend has had a bad fall. You want to drive him to the nearest hospital for emergency treatment. Which of these signs could be helpful?

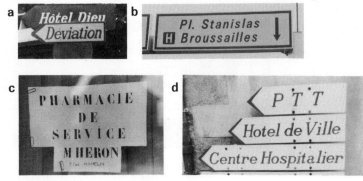

6 You've found the hospital. Which is the sign to the casualty department?

14 DANGERS AND EMERGENCIES

(See also chapter 13)

🔑 KEY WORDS

incendie (fire)	post (d') incendie fire point
secours (help)	poste de secours (first aid post) secours routier (roadside assistance) sortie de secours (emergency exit)
urgence (emergency)	secours d'urgence (emergency service) urgences (casualty department)

Steering clear of danger

A 'prohibition' sign (see p 7, 10) strengthened by **formellement, strictement, absolument** (strictly) or just **absolu,** is usually a warning that something is unsafe.

Danger means what it says: **danger de mort** or **danger mortel** tells you that life is at risk.

traverser to cross
sans utiliser signaux without using traffic lights

bains bathing
Côte Sauvage part of Brittany coast

You are alerted to lesser dangers by **attention** (beware) and **risque** (possible danger).

If things go wrong

You may have to find the emergency exit. Look for **sortie** (or **issue**) **de secours.**

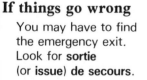

verglas icy roads

You may need police help and want to find a police station. In villages and small communities look for **gendarmerie** or **gendarmerie nationale,** in towns for **police** or **commissariat de police** (police station).

In Paris especially see if there's a police alarm (**avertisseur de police** or **secours de police**).

If you need first aid . . .

You'll need the casualty department (**urgences**) of a hospital (see p 91) unless you happen to spot a first aid post (**poste de secours**) nearby.

A **pharmacie** can sometimes help (see p 90).

C.R.S. = **Compagnies républicaines de sécurité** police responsible for public order

. . . or an ambulance

In case of accident or sudden illness call the fire brigade for an ambulance (see below). Otherwise phone the Red Cross (**Croix rouge**) or a local company, including some taxi companies, that provide **ambulances**.

To call the emergency services

. . . from a telephone

If you need the police or **gendarmerie** dial 17; in case of fire (**incendie**) or accident dial 18 for the fire brigade (**pompiers, sapeurs pompiers** or **service d'incendie**).
For an emergency call from a public phone you'll need a ½F, 1F or 5F coin, but your money will be returned.

. . . from the roadside

On major roads and motorways use the orange roadside phones marked **secours routier français**.

Elsewhere outside towns look for the
phone symbol and **gendarmerie**.
The words at the bottom of the sign
merely say who donated it – **don**
means gift, **prévention routière** road
safety i.e. prevention of road accidents.

Fire hazards

There is a real risk of forest fires during
hot weather in much of France.
Therefore open fires (**feux**) and
barbecues are often forbidden, for
instance, on camp sites.

allumer to light
en plein vent in the open air

TEST YOURSELF

1 Under what circumstances would these signs be important?

a SECOURS POLICE

PARLER ICI

b TÉLÉPHONE
INCENDIE
URGENCES

c *Commissariat Central*

d LA PREVENTION ROUTIERE
LA CROIX-ROUGE FRANCAISE
·POSTE
DE SECOURS
DON DE LA PREVENTION ROUTIERE

2 Which of these numbers would you call
  (i) if there's a burglary
  (ii) in case of fire
  (iii) if there's been an accident?

EN CAS D'URGENCE

POMPIERS   TEL. 18

GENDARMERIE TEL. 17

3 This is written on a roadside phone. What does it tell you?

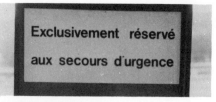

Exclusivement réservé aux secours d'urgence

4 Why should you not park here?

a

SORTIE
SAPEURS · POMPIERS

b

SORTIE de SECOURS
INTERDICTION
DE STATIONNER
A TOUS VÉHICULES

5 These signs are on a camp site. What is their message?

a

LES FEUX DE BOIS
SONT STRICTEMENT
INTERDITS
SOUS PEINE D'AMENDE

b

CONSIGNES d'INCENDIE (AR.Préf. 13.11.78)
Téléphone POMPIERS : 18
Ne pas crier au feu, alerter la Direction.

Answers to 'Test Yourself' Questions

Finding your way through the forest of signs

and 2 (Words in brackets give you the clue to the signs.)

(i) **e** 'close the door' (**fermer**); (ii) **d** 'ring please' (**s.v.p.**); (iii) **f** 'don't push, run and smoke' (**ne pas**); (iv) **b** 'entry prohibited' (**défense**) and **c** 'camping prohibited' (**interdit**); (v) **a** 'beware pickpockets' (**attention**).

and 4

(i) **e** 'way out'; (ii) **f** 'petrol station open'; (iii) **d** 'fierce dog'; (iv) **a** 'compulsory diversion' (i.e. you have to turn right); (v) **g** 'except religious services'; (vi) **b** 'extinguish your cigarette here' (vii) **c** 'exhibition − entry free of charge'.

a apply (**s'adresser**) at the Royal Gate; **b** wait (**attendre**) for a salesgirl (**vendeuse**); **c** don't smoke (**fumer**); **d** don't park (**stationner**); **e** close (**fermer**) the door; **f** don't cross (**traversez**).

---

1 office; prohibition; exit; road along a waterfront. 2 (i) on the right − straight on; (ii) step − market; (iii) square − beach; (iv) harbour − gate or door. 3 **a** Jean Bouin sports centre, town hall; **b** town centre, beaches, camp site 1.4 kms; **c** town hall, post office; **d** caretaker on 1st floor; **e** private road, cul-de-sac. 4 **a** enter without knocking; **b** pedestrians press and wait for the signal 'cross'; **c** pull. 5 **a** and **c**; **a** don't walk on the grass; **c** don't go through (i.e. no no way through for pedestrians) (**b** no entry for all vehicles). 6 **a** 30 metres on the left; **b** on the right at the end (**au fond**) of the yard. 7 when you're on foot looking for **a** way in to the car park; **b** castle; **c** harbour (**à 30m chemin de piétons** = footpath 30 metres ahead). 8 **a** by lift; **b** use the subway. 9 don't cross (**ne traversez pas**) if (**si**) the barriers are closed − a train is approaching (**arrive**). Innocent: this sign in Paris shows you the sightseeing route for pedestrians.

---

a 1 traffic; map; diversion; right of way; road; direction. 2 because of **a** children; **b** lorries emerging; **c** traffic from the right has priority when the light is flashing. 3 **a** police station, post office; **b** Invalides bridge and right bank; **c** lay-by (**veuve** means 'widow' − here the name of the locality). 4 **a** no entry 100 metres ahead; **b** end of one-way traffic; **c** single-lane road. 5 **a** give way; **b** drive in slowly and quietly, no noise please (**pas de** = no); **c** slow down (bad road surface for 7 kms; **nids de poules** = pot holes). 6 **a** pedestrians; **b** other traffic, not you. 7 **a** you can't go this way; **b** you'd be wise to follow the lorry route. 8 **a** relief road to Lisieux 400 metres ahead; **b** fast road to Brest; **c Route Nationale** (trunk road) to Paris.

---

1 coaches; motorised cycles; motorcycles. 2 **b** parking for cars; **d** for all vehicles (**a** coaches only; **c** heavy vehicles only; **e** hire cars only). 3 **a** free in August; **b** pay 8.30am − noon, 2pm − 6.30pm except Sundays and public holidays. 4 **a** and **b**; **a** restriction ends at 1pm; **b** no parking on Tuesday (**c** no parking for private cars Saturday 6am − 8pm). 5 vehicles parked in the pedestrian precinct will be towed away. 6 (i) **a** tells you to take a ticket from the 'pay and display' ticket machine, **b** points the way to the 'pay and display' car park; (ii) **a** two-wheelers must park here, **b** parking for light vehicles with back

wheels on pavement.   **7 a** cars, motorcycles, cycles park on dune side only;
b parking regulations in force;   **c** end of 'no parking'   **d** 'no waiting' on pavement.

c   1 automatic barrier; lane or queue; change or booth where you get change.
2 **a** exit for Mandelieu, La Napoule, Cannes, La Bocca;   **b** motorway police.
c slow vehicles keep to right hand lane;   **d** you're on the Eastern Motorway, tolls
levied from point 2 kms ahead.   3 **b** keep right (**a** you need 3F for left hand
lanes).   4 at Troarn exit there's a barrier where you pay the toll into a machine.

d   1 petrol; repairs of mechanical faults; petrol station.   2 (i) **b** (**a** is 2-stroke
mixture);   (ii) **b** (**a** is for air and water);   (iii) **a** (**b** oil change and lubrication);
(iv) **a** (**b** windscreens of all types fitted). Innocent: **aire** is a lay-by.

3   1 connections; driver; taxi rank.   2 **b** right hand side (**voyageurs sans ticket**) (**a** says
'no entry').   3 **RER** and underground lines 1, 2, 6.   4 change to line **Mairie
d'Ivry**.   5 **a** and **b** coaches;   **c** coaches and buses;   **d** railway and underground;
e underground.   6 **a** batches of bus and underground tickets, normal fare;
b supplementary tickets for travel to suburbs;   **c** all kinds of tickets for travel in Paris.
Innocent: **station taxis** marks the rank, not the destination.

4   1 date-stamp (your ticket); platform.   2 **b** (**SNCF**) (**a** bus station;   **c** boat
terminal).   3 (i) **a** (**consigne**);   (ii) **a** (**renseignements**);   (iii) **e**;   (iv) **c**;   (v) **b**;
(vi) **d**.   4 **b** (**a** exit only).   5 follow **b** luggage lockers (**a** left-luggage closed
midnight – 6am).   6 **a** date-stamping machine out of order (**en dérangement**), use
another machine (**autre appareil**);   **b** if you're with a passenger don't forget (**n'oubliez
pas**) your platform ticket.   7 **a** advertises car hire (**voitures** = cars or railway
carriages);   **b** shows order of train carriages.   8 **a** you can hire a self-drive car (**sans
chauffeur**);   **b** this way to the motorail sleeper;   **c** you can hire cycles at the luggage
counter. Innocent: **chariots** are luggage trolleys.

5   1 hotel; letting; full board; one-room flatlet.   2 **a** room-booking service;   **b** furnished
rooms and one-room flatlets to let.   3 **a** town hall (**b** and **c** are hotels).
4 **a** and **b** rooms with breakfast;   **c** rooms;   **d** bar offering furnished rooms and meals.
5 no, the site is full.   6 **a** sink for vegetables;   **b** washbasins;   **c** dustbins;
d reception. Innocent: not a hotel, but the former military hospital in Paris, now a
museum and national monument.

6   1 phone box; mail.   2 (i) **a**;   (ii) neither (**a** for calls inside France,   **b** for local
calls).   3 printed matter.   4 (i) **b** the key word is **affranchissement** (**a** is for large
amounts of stamps, (**timbres en gros**), and for collections, **avion** is airmail);   (ii) **b** the
key word is **recommandation** (= registered mail).   5 **a** opening hours of post office
and collection times;   **b** camp site letterbox: mail collection between (**entre**) 10 and
12.

7   1 bank note; currency exchange; bank; small change; coin.   2 no   **a** 'counter
closed';   **b** closed between noon and 2 pm.   3 **b** and **e** (**a** finance company,
c savings bank,   **d** counter for getting change).   4 change for 10 franc notes.
5 (i) put in 1 franc (you get 5 20-centimes coins);   (ii) insert exact coinage to make up
13 francs. Innocent: **monnaie** means small change.

8   1 route round a particular area; old town; places of interest; exhibition; old town house,
historic building; palace, large hall, or name of modern block of flats; tower or tour.
2 **a** old town;   **b** wine cellar of tourist interest;   **c** way to gardens;   **d** beautiful view
of the town and the river Loire (**les Chatelliers**, a name);   **e** tourist route.   3 **a** and **b**
(**c** is a travel agency).   4 **a, b, d** (**aquarelles** = watercolours, **sur soie** = on silk) (**c** is
a wine cellar,   **e** a restaurant garden).   5 **a** route through the cider-producing areas;

b Laon, its town walls, abbeys, chapel of the Templars, museum (**son, sa, ses** = its);
c park called **Bel-Air** and public gardens. 6 **b** tour of old town and castle (**a** trip round the lake, **c** visit to Savonnières caves). 7 **a** and **b** every day.
8 (i) unaccompanied children under 13 not admitted; (ii) Sundays and public holidays; (iii) yes. Innocent: **caves** = wine cellars.

---

1 ball; small boat; hire; trip or ride. 2 **b** (a difficult path (**roches** = rocks, **parcours** = route), impassable in winter (**impraticable en hiver**), **c** path for hikers). 3 **b** and **c** (**a** is boat hire). 4 **a** no waiting; **b** no cycling on pavement; **c** prohibited for motorised cycles and motorcycles. 5 **a** and **b** (**c** bathing forbidden).
6 **a** motorboats, rowing boats and pedal boats (for hire); **b** sailboards for hire and for sale (**vente**); **c** motorboat tour of the lake; **d** no bathing from (**depuis**) small boats.
7 **a** ball games forbidden in the square; **b** nursery, free playground; **c** place for playing bowls. Innocent: **golf** is mis-spelt here; it should be **golfe** = bay; (**jeux de plage** = beach games; the rest of the sign advertises changing facilities, chairs, parasols, drinks, sweets, ice-creams).

---

0 1 special offer; wine shop or wine cellar; suits; shop selling household articles, hardware, toiletries etc.; bookshop; special offer; department; sales. 2 (i) **b** (a horse butcher's); (ii) **a** (**b** food department only); (iii) **b** (a clothes shop); (iv) **b** (a means you can go in and look around). 3 **d** for insecticide; **a** and probably **f** for eggs and butter; **b** for postcards and stamps; **c** for sandals; **e** for wine; **f** for crisps and biscuits. 4 **a** fruit and (early) vegetables; **b** groceries, vegetables, dairy products, frozen food household articles etc., crockery. 5 **a** end-of-sale, no price increase (**vite** = quickly); **b** special offer; **c** the week's special offer; **d** special offer, exceptional sale. 6 **a** no exit without purchase; **b** cash desk; **c** pay for your purchases before leaving (**avant de quitter**) the basement. 7 (i) **c**; (ii) **a**; (iii) **b** (but not for men!). Innocent: **prix choc** = amazing value, 50 = 50 articles.

---

1 1 menu; cold; ice-cream parlour; set menu; flavour; dish; fish. 2 when you're in a hurry (i.e. quick meals). 3 Italian spaghetti, sausages, grilled steak or roast chicken with chips. 4 **a** self-service; **b** inn; **c** tea room (**pâtisserie** sells cakes and pastries, **traiteur** is a caterer). 5 **a** cold drinks, sandwiches, ice-creams; **b** cooked meats, prepared dishes; **c** selection of (**variées**) barbecued skewered meat, grills, chips; **d** grills, Italian specialities, pancakes galore (**à gogo**); **e** spit-roast chicken (**fermier** = from the farm, **broche** = spit). 6 **a** they sell tobacco, postcards, stamps etc. and take bets; **b** they serve snacks all day. 7 **b** and **c** the key words are **à emporter** and **portatives** (**a** make ice-cream on the premises (**maison**)). Innocent: **croque monsieur** is a toasted sandwich (**croquer** = to munch or crunch).

---

2 1 **c** (**a** men, **b** closed, **d** private, **e** gents). 2 **a** loos, telephone, drinks and chips; **b** charge for loo ½F and for showers 3F; **c** loos for men and women, urinal and shoe cleaning.

---

3 1 hospital; doctor; emergency. 2 **b** (a dentist specialising in orthodontics, **c** GP). 3 (i) in an emergency and by appointment; (ii) during surgery hours daily 8.30 am to 12 and by appointment. 4 **b** (**a** is a doctor). 5 **a**, **b** and **d** (**c** tells you which chemist's is on duty (**de service**)). 6 **a** (**b** out-patients). Innocent: **clinique du pneu** is a tyre mending service.

---

4 1 **a** and **c** if you needed police help. **b** to phone the fire brigade or emergency services; **d** to get first aid. 2 (i) 17; (ii) 18; (iii) 17 or 18. 3 reserved for calling emergency services. 4 **a** exit for fire engine; **b** emergency exit.
5 **a** wood fires strictly prohibited on penalty of a fine (**sous peine d'amende**); **b** in case of fire dial 18, don't panic (**crier au feu**), inform the management (**direction**).

Word List

The meanings listed here apply to words used on the signs included in this book; other meanings are not listed. The numbers in brackets refer you to the page on which the word is explained more fully. Words where the meaning is obvious are omitted.

à at, to, for
abbaye abbey
absolu(ment) strict(ly)
accompagné accompanied; guided
accôtement verge
accueil welcome; reception
    de France tourist office
achat purchase
affaire offer
affranchissement postage stamps
aire lay-by, service area
alimentation food shop, department, groceries
aller-retour return ticket
alterné alternate
ancien old; former
animaux animals
ans years
août August
appareil machine; (petrol) pump
appartements flats
appuyer, appuyez press; lean
après after
arrêt stop
arrière rear, back
ascenseur lift
assiette plate
attendez wait
attendre to wait (for)
attention beware
au(x) to the, for the, at the, on the
auberge inn
auto car
autobus bus
autocar coach, bus (38)
automatique automatic; automatic barrier
autorisé permitted
autoroute motorway

autre other
avant before
avec with
avez: vous avez you have

bac sink
bagages luggage
baignade bathing
baigner to bathe
bains baths; bathing
ballon ball
banlieue suburb
banque bank
bar bar etc. (83)
barque rowing boat
barré closed off
bateau boat
beau, bel(le) fine, beautiful
bilateral on both sides
billet ticket; (bank) note
bis secondary; 'a' (12)
bld. = boulevard
bleu blue
bois wood
boisson drink
boîte box
boucherie butcher's
boulangerie baker's
boules bowls
bouton button
brasserie café-cum-restaurant (82)
brochettes skewered meat
bruit noise
buffet (de gare) station restaurant
bureau office; reception
    d'accueil reception office
    de tourisme tourist office
buvette kiosk selling drinks

c. = centime(s)
cabine phone box; cubicle
cabinet office; cubicle
caddie supermarket trolley

caisse cash desk; cashier's; checkout
    d'épargne savings bank
camion lorry
campeur camper
camping camp site, camping
canot à moteur motorboat
car (autocar) coach, bus
carnet booklet, batch (of tickets)
carte menu; map
    postale postcard
cas: en cas de in case of
casse-croûte snack
cave, caveau wine cellar, wine shop
ce, cette this
cédez give way
centre town centre; centre
    hospitalier hospital
    ville town centre
cérémonies services
chambres rooms
    d'hôte bed and breakfast
change(s) currency exchange
changeur money-changing machine
chantier building site; road works
charcuterie cooked meats
chariot luggage trolley, supermarket trolley
château castle; palace; country house
chauffé heated
chaussée roadway; road surface
chaussures shoes
chemin road, footpath
cher expensive
chevaline (boucherie chevaline) horse butcher's

chien dog
chirurgien-dentiste dentist
choc shock
choix choice
circuit route round a
   particular place
circulation traffic
circuler to drive, ride
cireur shoe-cleaner
cité old part of a town
cl. = classe quality class
clignotant flashing
climatisé air-conditioned
coiffeur hairdresser
coiffure hairdressing
comestibles foods
comme like
commissariat de police
   police station
complet full
composter to date-stamp
composteur date-stamping
   machine
compostez date-stamp
compris included
concièrge caretaker
conducteur driver
confection clothes,
   fashions
confiserie confectionery
conseillé recommended,
   alternative
consigne left luggage;
   instructions
   automatique left luggage
   lockers
consultations surgery
   hours
consultations externes
   out-patients
contrôlé checked;
   registered
corail fast inter-city
   train (44)
cordonnerie shoemaker's
correspondance con-
   nection; correspondance
costume suit
côte coast
côté side
cour yard
courir to run
courrier post, mail

crédit bank; credit
crèmerie dairy
crêpe pancake
crêperie pancake house
crier to shout
croix cross; intersection
croque monsieur toasted
   sandwich (82)
cts. = centimes
cuisine kitchen; cooking
cuisiné ready cooked
curiosité place of interest
cyclable, cycliste for
   cyclists
cyclo (cyclomoteur)
   motorised cycle

D = route départementale
   (19)
d' = de
dames
   women, ladies
dans in
de of, from; to
défendu prohibited
défense prohibition
déformé bad, damaged
dégustation sampling,
   tasting (84)
déjeuner lunch
délestage relief route
demander to ask (for)
demi half
départ departure; (mail)
   collection
dérangement: en dérange-
   ment out of order
dernier last
des of the
descente exit from vehicle
détail small quantities
devant in front of
déviation diversion
dimanche Sunday
direction management;
   direction, route
disponible available
disposition disposal
disque parking disc (27, 28)
distributeur machine for
   dispensing cash, tickets
distribution automatique
   ticket machine

docteur (Dr) doctor (90)
douche shower
droguerie shop selling
   hardware, household
   goods etc.
droit fee; straight
droite right
du of the

eau water
échange de monnaie place
   where you get small
   change
église church
embarcadère landing stage
embarcation small boat
emporter to take away
en in, on, into
enfants children
enlèvement removal,
   towing away
entrée entry, entrance; fee
   libre entry free of
   charge; come in and
   look around
entrer to enter
entrer, entrez enter
entresol floor between
   ground level and 1st
   floor
épicerie grocer's
escalier stairs
essence petrol; 2-star
   petrol
est east; is
et and
étage floor, storey
été summer
éteignez extinguish
étranger abroad; foreign
   (counter)
exclusivement exclusively
exposition (expo) exhibition

F = franc(s)
faire, faites make
   l'appoint insert correct
   money
   signe signal
femmes women
ferme farm
fermé closed
fermer, fermez close

fermeture closing
fête public holiday
feu fire; (traffic) light
file lane, queue
fin end
formellement strictly
frais, fraîche chilled, fresh
frapper to knock
friterie stall or shop selling fried food
frites, pommes frites chips
frs. = **francs**
fruits de mer seafood
fumer to smoke
fumeur smoker

garage de vélos cycle shed
garder to keep
garderie d'enfants nursery
gardez keep
gare station
  maritime boat terminal
  routière coach station
gauche left
gênant causing obstruction
gendarmerie police (station)
gîte rural dwelling (50)
glace ice, ice-cream
glacier ice-cream parlour
graissage lubrication
grand great; main
gratuit free of charge
grillades grills
gros large, bulky
  en gros in large quantities
grotte cave
guichet counter

H = **heure** hour
h, H = **hôpital**
halles covered market
hebdomadaire weekly
heure (h, H) hour; time
hommes men
horaire times; timetable
horodateur 'pay & display' ticket machine
hors out of
hostellerie hotel
hôtel hotel; town house (48)

de ville town hall
Dieu hospital
huile oil

ici here
il it
impasse dead end
impraticable unsuitable
imprimés printed matter
incendie fire
interdiction prohibition
interdit prohibited
interurbain (for) inland (phone calls)
introduction insert coins
introduire to bring in; insert
introduisez insert
issue exit
itinéraire route

jardin garden (63)
jeu game
jeudi Thursday
jeunesse youth
jour day
  férié public holiday
journaux newspapers
journée whole day
  continue open all day

la the
lac lake
lavabos washbasins
lavage car wash
laver to wash
le(s) the; on
léger light
légumes vegetables
lent(ement) slow(ly)
levée mail collection
librairie bookshop
libre free of charge; vacant, available
  service self-service
ligne line, route, service
linge clothes
livraisons deliveries
livre pound, 500g; book
location hire, letting
louer let, hire
lundi Monday

m = **mètre**
mairie town hall
maison house; home-made
mandat money order
marchandise goods
marché market
marche step
marcher to walk
mardi Tuesday
marque make
mécanique mechanical faults
méchant fierce
médecin doctor (90)
mélange mixture
ménage household goods
menu fixed price meal
mer sea
merci thank you
mercredi Wednesday
messieurs men, gents
métro underground railway
mettez insert
meublé furnished; furnished room
midi noon
minuit midnight
minute 'while you wait'
moins (de) less (than); under
monnaie (small) change; booth where you get change (33, 57)
montée entrance to vehicle
monument (historic) building
mort death
moto (motocycle) motor cycle
musée museum

N **route nationale** (19);
  n' = **ne**
nature type; plain
no = **numéro** number
ne pas, ne . . . pas don't, no
nettoyage cleaning
nocturne late-night
non no; not
nos, notre our

nuit night

obligatoire compulsory
occupé engaged
ordinaire 2-star petrol
ou or
ouvert open
ouverture opening
ouvrable working (day)
ouvrir to open

palais palace, large hall (62)
panier basket
panne breakdown
par by, via
parc park; car park (29)
  de jeux playground
pare-brise windscreen
parfum perfume; flavour
parfumerie shop selling toiletries, cosmetics etc.
parking car park
parler speak
pas walking pace; **pas de** no
passage way through; right of way
  souterrain subway
passez go, cross
pâtisserie cake shop; cakes and pastries
payant you have to pay
payer to pay
payez insert money; pay
pays country
  du pays locally produced
péage toll
pédalo pedal boat
pédestre on foot, for pedestrians
peinture painting
pelouse lawn
pension board and lodging
peser to weigh
petit small, little
  déjeuner breakfast
pharmacie dispensing chemist's
pièce coin; room; each
piéton pedestrian
piétonne, piétonnier for pedestrians

piscine swimming pool
piste track
pl. = place, PL = poids lourds
place square
places spaces; seats
plage beach
planches à voile sailboards
plat dish; food
plein full
pneu tyre
poids lourds (PL) heavy or long vehicles
poisson fish
pommes de terre potatoes
pompiers fire brigade
pont bridge
port harbour
portative take-way
porte door, gate
poste post office; post
potable fit to drink
poubelle dustbin
poulet chicken
pour for; in order to
pousser, poussez push
prendre to take
prenez take
pression draught
prêt-à-porter ready-to-wear fashions
prié requested
prière de please
primeurs early vegetables
prioritaire something that has right of way
priorité right of way
privé private; individual
prix price(s) (74)
profitez take advantage
promenade walk, trip, ride
promotion (promo) special offer
PTT post office (52)

quai station platform; road along a waterfront
quartier part, area
quitter to leave

ralentissez slow down
randonnée ramble

rapide fast train; coach; quick
rappel reminder
rayon department (in shop)
réclame special offer
recommandé recommended, alternative; registered (mail)
réduit reduced
refroidi frozen
régie local government control
régionaux regional
réglages car tuning
réglementé controlled, restricted
réglez pay (for)
relais roadside inn
remparts town walls
rendez-vous appointment
rendu returned
renseignements information
repas meal
réseau network
retour return
rive bank
rôti roast
roue wheel
rouge red
roulez drive
route (rte) road; route
routier road . . .
routiers transport drivers (82)
rte = route
rue street

s. = siècle
s' = se or **si**
sac bag
s'adresser ask, apply, call
salle room, hall
  d'attente waiting room
salon hairdresser's
  de thé tea room
samedi Saturday
sanisette, sanitaire loo
sans without
sapeurs pompiers fire brigade
saucisse sausage
sauf except

sauvage wild
se itself, oneself, yourself
secours emergency; help;
first-aid
semaine week
sens direction
interdit no entry
unique one-way
sentier footpath
serrez keep
seulement only
si if
siècle (s.) century
s'il vous plaît (s.v.p.)
please
site place of historic
interest
SNCF French Railways
soins treatment
solde sales
so ne nnez ring
s are
ez drive out
rtie exit; trip
de secours emergency
exit
sous-sol basement
souterrain underground
stade sports centre,
stadium
station taxi rank; petrol
station
stationnement (stat!)
parking
stationner to park
stationnez park
studio one-room flatlet
super = supercarburant
4-star petrol
supermarché supermarket
sur for, on, by

surgelé(s) frozen food
surveillé supervised
s.v.p. = s'il vous plaît
please
syndicat d'initiative tourist
office

tabac tobacco;
tobacconist's (74, 83)
talon heel
tarif charge, fee, price;
fare
taxiphone phone for local
calls
ticket de caisse receipt
timbres stamps
-poste postage stamps
tirer, tirez pull
titres de transport tickets
toilette loo; personal
hygiene; wash and
brush up
toléré permissible
tour tower; (round) trip
tourisme touring,
tourist. . .
touristique of tourist
interest, for tourists
tourner to turn
tous all, every
tout any, every
droit straight on
traiteur caterer
travaux road works
traverser to cross
traversez cross
trottoir pavement

un, une a
unique one, single

urgence emergency
urgences emergency
treatment; casualty
department
urinoir urinal
utiliser use
utilitaire commercial

vacances holidays
vaisselle crockery
vedette motor launch
véhicules de tourisme
private cars
vélo cycle
vélomoteur moped
vendredi Friday
vente sale
vérifier to check
vers towards
vert green
vidange oil-change
vieux, vieil(le) old
ville town
vin wine
visite sightseeing tour; visit
visiter to visit
visiteurs visitors
voie way, road; lane of a
road; railway line;
station platform (44)
voile sail
voiliers sailing boats
voiture car (19,26);
railway carriage
volailles poultry
vos, votre your
vous you
voyage trip
voyageur passenger